"*Flyover Church* is yet another reason why I'm so thankful for Brad Roth's pastoring and writing. This book is full of arresting stories, nuanced insights, and fresh and faithful readings of the Scriptures—all expressed in beautifully written, memorable prose. Here is a Harvard-trained pastor who loves Jesus and bales hay. This book is indeed the 'lean yet weighty' volume that Brad aspired to write. Read it for pleasure and profit."

STEPHEN WITMER, pastor of Pepperell Christian Fellowship, council member of The Gospel Coalition, and author of *A Big Gospel in Small Places*

"In this book, Brad Roth opens the soul of the small-town pastor, describing our struggles and challenges, not to cause us to abandon ministry but to give us hope and perspective by helping us understand ourselves and the communities we serve. Writing with personal reflection, insightful research, and theological clarity, Roth gives us insight into what it means to be a rural pastor. Like his previous book *God's Country*, this book is invaluable and is on the must-read shelf of books on rural ministry."

GLENN DAMAN, author of *The Forgotten Church, When Shepherds Weep*, and *The Lighthouse: Discovering Security in the Radiance of God's Character*

"With his inimitable writing style, Brad Roth weaves snapshots from Christ's time on earth (as the quintessential rural minister) with snippets of wisdom and insights gleaned from his and other pastors' decades of rural living and ministry. *Flyover Church* is a beautiful tapestry that is compelling, authentic, vulnerable, and hopeful."

RON KLASSEN, executive director emeritus of the Rural Home Missionary Association

"*Flyover Church* is a gift to the whole church. Brad Roth offers a compelling portrait of rural churches, a portrait whose beauty is drawn from the hope and hardships of ministry in rural places. This book offers important truths about the rural church, and in doing so reminds us that these congregations are full of deep and meaningful ministries."

ALLEN T. STANTON, consulting fellow at University of the Ozarks and author of *Reclaiming Rural: Building Thriving Rural Congregations*

"With an artist's pen, Brad Roth engages the reader's imagination in *Flyover Church*. His love for the ways of Jesus and how they can be experienced in rural ministry provide a treasure of wisdom. I highly recommend this book as a rich source of encouragement for those in small places."

DAVID PINCKNEY, regional director for Acts 29

flyover church

flyover church

HOW JESUS' MINISTRY IN RURAL PLACES IS GOOD NEWS EVERYWHERE

Brad Roth

HERALD
P R E S S

Harrisonburg, Virginia

Herald Press
PO Box 866, Harrisonburg, Virginia 22803
www.HeraldPress.com

Library of Congress Cataloging-in-Publication Data
Names: Roth, Brad, author.
Title: Flyover church : how Jesus' ministry in rural places is good news
    everywhere / Brad Roth.
Description: Harrisonburg, Virginia : Herald Press, [2024] | Includes
    bibliographical references.
Identifiers: LCCN 2024011614 (print) | LCCN 2024011615 (ebook) | ISBN
    9781513813721 (paperback) | ISBN 9781513813738 (hardcover) | ISBN
    9781513813745 (ebook)
Subjects: LCSH: Rural clergy. | Rural churches. | Rural population. |
    BISAC: RELIGION / Christian Ministry / Pastoral Resources | RELIGION /
    Christian Theology / Ecclesiology
Classification: LCC BV638.7 .R67 2024 (print) | LCC BV638.7 (ebook) | DDC
    253.09173/4--dc23/eng/20240516
LC record available at https://lccn.loc.gov/2024011614
LC ebook record available at https://lccn.loc.gov/2024011615

Study guides are available for many Herald Press titles at www.HeraldPress.com.

FLYOVER CHURCH
© 2024 by Bradley A. Roth
Released by Herald Press, Harrisonburg, Virginia 22803. 800-245-7894. All rights reserved.
Library of Congress Control Number: 2024011614
International Standard Book Number: 978-1-5138-1372-1 (paperback);
    978-1-5138-1373-8 (hardcover); 978-1-5138-1374-5 (ebook)
Printed in United States of America

28 27 26 25 24   10 9 8 7 6 5 4 3 2 1

To Lici, Mateo, Elijah, and Pablo

Contents

Foreword

"Flyover country" is a uniquely North American term. The vast amount of land in the United States and Canada requires fast, efficient means of transportation, so air travel is more common in North America than anywhere else. A quick Google search shows that the United States and Canada (ranked first and fourth) have more airports than the next twenty-five countries combined.

That's a *lot* of flyover country. And a lot of flyover churches. This has created three challenges:

First, the cities we fly into get a lot more attention than the towns we fly over. So there's a much higher concentration of church leadership advice from and for city-based ministries than rural ones. Most seminaries are adjacent to cities with airports, and we hold church leadership conferences there as well.

This is not unreasonable. Gathering at population hubs makes sense. I'm not suggesting we move all colleges to small towns or hold conferences in agricultural regions. But we need to be more purposeful about the needs of small-town churches, and we need to hear from rural pastors. Big-city ideas and methods seldom translate to places where land is more often measured in acres than square feet.

Second, we tend to use the culture and values of city-based churches to gauge the success and effectiveness of all churches. This is a huge shift. It wasn't long ago that stereotypical "American values" (a nebulous term, for sure) came primarily from the breadbasket states, not the cities. From Smallville, not Metropolis.

As you'll read in these pages, rural ministry isn't just done at a different *scale* from city and suburban ministry, it has a different pace, a different way of measuring success, and requires a very different set of pastoral gifts and skills. But it's hard for us to value these differences when city-based ministry is our default.

Third, rural regions aren't purposely ignored as much as they're unintentionally forgotten. No one spontaneously goes to or through rural places anymore. I'm old enough that our family car trips traveled *through* cities like Wheeling, West Virginia; Evansville, Indiana; and Tucumcari, New Mexico, instead of *above* and *around* them. Hotels were in the middle of town, not a string of cookie-cutter chain hotels lining the interstate.

Because I work with small churches, I often speak in rural communities. On a recent flight, the plane flew over the town I was heading toward, and I spotted the building where the meeting would be held. It was so close that the distance was measured in feet, not miles (about twenty thousand feet directly overhead, but still . . . feet). But to travel that very short distance, I had to complete my flight and then drive over two hundred miles. So close, but so far.

That's what rural ministry is like. These communities are so close, but so far. And not just geographically. The cultural differences between urban and rural communities are even more stark. Flying over towns or driving around them has given us speed and efficiency, but it has also changed our perspective—and not in a good way. We look down on small towns and rural regions, literally and figuratively. Compared to the bustling cities we fly into, rural places are an afterthought, if they're thought of at all.

The body of Christ needs to think more deeply than this. We're not only called to population-dense cities and suburbs; we're also called to the fringes. Like Ruth, we must find our place among the gleaners in Boaz's field, working alongside those who follow behind, rescuing the forgotten, and foraging in the overlooked corners of society. Like Jesus, we mustn't forget the smaller populations in the rural fields of Galilee while we minister in the crowded streets of Jerusalem.

In this book, Brad Roth provides many helpful insights for how to think differently, measure success more accurately, and minister more effectively in rural settings. Whether you serve in a rural area or, like me, in a highly populated city or suburb, knowing more about flyover churches and the people who worship and serve in them will help us all.

> —**Karl Vaters**, author of several books,
> including *De-Sizing the Church: How
> Church Growth Became a Science,
> Then an Obsession, and What's Next*

1

The Beginning and Baptism

The beginning of the good news of Jesus Christ, the Son of God. —Mark 1:1

It was summer, and I was cruising with my family in our old pickup truck along the main street of our rural Kansas community. We had crossed the train tracks and rounded a bend, when a man we didn't know stepped out from his front door. We gave him the requisite Wave. Of course he waved back. But then he surprised us by calling out: "We're still here!"

It was 2021, and that was the cry of his mid-pandemic heart. After all that had transpired, we're still breathing, dreaming, living. We're still here! But that shout hung with me like a metaphor of something more. It rang in my ears like the story of rural North America in the past decade or so: We're still here!

And we are. Depending on how you count, some sixty million people (nearly 20 percent of the total population) call rural America home.[1] Statistics Canada counts a similar percentage of the overall population living in rural Canada—a number that will undoubtedly be found to have shrunk when the latest data is released.[2] Despite its enormous land mass, Canada's population is more urbanized than in the United States. The majority of the rural population of the Great White North also clusters within commuting distance of large urban areas.[3] Still, rural life runs differently than life in Toronto and Tulsa, Montreal and Minneapolis.

By our very nature, we rural people are spread out. There's no one rural state or province. Pick any dense metropolis—New York, Philadelphia, Chicago, Denver—and you'll discover rural swathes feeding the suburbs and exurbs and ring-road villages. And population density plays a role in defining rural. It's not just that there are fewer people. It's also that there's more space between them.

As a percentage of the overall population in the United States, rural would seem to have experienced a century of decline as urban and suburban areas swelled. Yet in absolute terms, rural is holding its own or possibly growing.[4]

The story of the rural church tracks many of the same trend lines of broader population shifts. Smaller families and educational and economic aspirations mean that many rural congregations are missing the twenty- and thirty-something set as young people hit the road for college and never come back.

That was my family's story.

My grandparents attended a tiny rural Mennonite congregation at the edge of a field across from a seed plant—a church they played a role in founding in their young married farmer days. My parents hauled us kids to special events at that country church. I remember running in the plain cement basement. But it was not the church I grew up in. My parents chose a much larger congregation with a youth pastor and scads of programs. I was deeply formed by growing up in that big church. The teaching and experiences gave me an enduring love for the Bible and an evangelistic outlook. But my family was part of a shift away from small family churches in the country toward larger congregations in central communities.[5] Eventually, my grandparents' congregation closed its doors for good—though they sold the building to a King-James-only Baptist congregation that has been making a go of it.

I left the farm for college and then pushed on to the East Coast and graduate school. I wasn't fleeing rural so much as seeking opportunity (though I didn't mind getting away from baling hay). So far, so conventional. But somewhere along the way, I got married and got called, and my wife and I found ourselves back in the Midwest as I studied for the ministry. A congregation in eastern Washington State took a chance on me and invited me to come be their pastor. After that, we served as missionaries to congregations in the rural Andes of the Cusco region of Peru. And then, because God is good and generous, we were called to rural Kansas.

I didn't set out to become a rural pastor. I just wanted to serve the church. But here I am.

I've ended up living in rural places most of my life. Over the past couple of years, I've sought to listen deeply and learn about the challenges that rural communities and congregations face. Part of what I've found is that they're common challenges, whatever our distinctive theologies—charismatic to Catholic.

But more importantly, I have discovered over and again the common promise of the gospel. Jesus vowed that the gates of Hades will never prevail against the church (Matthew 16:18). He's literally with it through hell and high water. As the apostle Peter wrote in his second letter, Christ has given us "everything we need for living a godly life" (2 Peter 1:3 NLT). This is a promise for the rural church—and small churches wherever they may be found—and we need to hear it and claim it for our own now more than ever: Christ has given us everything we need.

Over the past several years, interest in rural people and places swelled. In the wake of the 2016 US election, intrepid city folks ventured out of the coastal metropolises to gaze at rural people. Who are they? What do they want? The musings of these urban observers, some of them rural émigré explainers, spawned a new literary genre: the "redneck safari."[6] Rural, it seemed, was having its moment.

Until it wasn't.

The impulse to listen and understand, originally urgent in 2016, became embittered and impatient in certain circles by the 2020 election in the United States. Outside opinion reverted to form, seeing rural as a backward, embittered, monochrome, children-of-the-corn kind of place where people cling to their guns and religion.[7] It wasn't long before most of the inland anthropologists had skipped town and jetted back to the city.

So too, over the past few years the broader church has remembered its rural congregations again for the first time and began to ask how prevailing models of church and mission fit (or didn't) in rural communities. Since 2016, multiple parachurch organizations have been created to equip rural pastors and leaders, including the Rural Matters Institute out of Wheaton College. These new initiatives have come alongside long-standing organizations like the Rural Home Missionary Association and Village Missions. A basket of helpful books have also been released, including Donnie Griggs's *Small Town Jesus*, Stephen Witmer's *Big Gospel in Small Places*, Allen T. Stanton's *Reclaiming Rural*, and Glenn Daman's *The Forgotten Church*. And my own *God's Country*. It's welcome attention and resourcing.

Because however much national and ecclesial attention may flicker on to something else, rural communities and congregations persist. Rurality isn't a problem to be solved. Rural is a way of life, a kind of culture. We're still here.

But where are we, and what are we doing here?

WHERE AM I?

Where am I? and *What am I doing here?* are pretty much the first two questions I asked myself after I plopped down behind my desk in my office cubby on the backside of my first, small rural church in eastern Washington, summer 2006. "Can you get any farther away?" my parents asked after we bundled their (then) lone grandson into the car and made for the western horizon. "Look at it this way," I said. "At least you don't need a passport."

Our town was majority Spanish-speaking, the strata of community built up after irrigation water hit the high desert from the federal Grand Coulee Dam project and intensive farming became possible. We were the newbies in a town with roots that sank deep into the sagebrush hills. We didn't know a soul beyond our congregation, and we were only just getting to know them. Every industrial clunk and shudder woke us in the night. We peaked through the blinds onto an alien midnight landscape.

We began to love place and people once we began to know them. It took a few years. With every birthday party and graduation and quinceañera, we plotted our topography of ministry. Summer, autumn, winter, spring. Potato and onion and cherry harvest. Alfalfa tucked into great round bales. The seasons marked our lives. Doors into the community began to crack open.

Perhaps rural ministry requires a deeper and more committed knowledge of place than other kinds of ministry. It's impossible to do the work of the church without first surveying the lay of the land. There's no one way to be rural. For instance, rural Alaska with its unsleeping summers, dark, weary winters, and rhythms of hunting and fishing is quite different from the rural Great Plains with miles of wheat, corn, soybeans, and milo.

Rural can be defined in multiple ways. Population plays a key role, both in total numbers and in density. Several long-standing government categories define rural as indicating communities of less than twenty-five hundred people with a density of no more than one thousand people per square mile.[8] Agriculture also plays a role in a rural identity, if nothing else than by its high visibility. Surprisingly few rural people work directly in agriculture. While you might be rural if the tallest building in town is the grain elevator, ubiquitous on the Great Plains and across the Corn Belt, rural economies are often quite diversified, particularly if they've had the good luck to be located on an interstate highway within range of a city.

Rural communities trend older, with a median age of fifty-one compared to forty-five in urban areas.[9] Many of the rural communities in my swath of central Kansas boast fine retirement villages and nursing homes, making them a destination for retirees. This means a tremendous pool of accumulated wisdom in our communities, though the trend can also skew the town's priorities, like when it's time to pass a school bond (we got our latest $14 million bond passed on the third try).

Rural areas can be surprisingly diverse. Garden City in western Kansas (a micropolitan community of over thirty thousand people—admittedly larger than most rural definitions) boasts some twenty languages spoken in the local school.[10] Wherever you find meat-packing plants across the Midwest and Great Plains, you'll find strong immigrant communities from Latin America, Asia, and Africa. Once, on a visit to a community of six thousand in central Nebraska, I dropped into the Mexican grocery store and passed two young Somali women wearing hijabs on their way out the door. That's rural too.

But beyond statistical designations, rural is a way of seeing the world. Sociologist Robert Wuthnow calls rural a "moral community." This is not to say that rural places are moral while suburbs or cities are immoral.[11] Rather, the language of "moral community" indicates how rural communities have a common identity that they understand themselves by.

Rural is characterized by being a known and knowable community. Particularly in communities under twenty-five hundred, it's often possible to place everyone on the family tree—or at least to believe that you can place them. We know each other out here, and people know us. You go for a walk and expect to see people you know. If there's a disaster, like a house fire, you expect to know about it and help out the family. There are formal responsibilities and contracts and job obligations in rural communities just like there are in cities and suburbs, but what really sets rural apart are the informal obligations and relationships that bind people together. Rural is the kind of place where you leave your car in the drive with the keys in it for the mechanic to pick up, change the oil, and return. He leaves the bill on the seat. Once, in a rush, I left a gallon of milk in the back seat of my car, and in my absence the mechanic let himself into the house to put the milk in the fridge. That kind of thing is what gives rural communities their distinctive culture and character. Thus the dissonance when large-scale population changes occur, like when a multi-national food processor builds a plant in town and attracts a

new and diverse workforce—or when that plant shutters and
the workers leave.

But there's also a danger in talking about "rural." Contemporary American rural identity hasn't always existed. It was
created over time by a cluster of cultural forces, including the
government, media, and economic shifts. Rural is not an enduring and settled identity. The 1920 US Census documented for
the first time more people living in urban areas than rural.[12]
Before that, rural Americans were mostly just Americans, and
rural was something of a synonym for *local*. As sociologists
Nicholas Jacobs and Daniel Shea write, it took at least another
sixty years of populism, agrarian movements, and the 1980s
farm crisis—an economic catastrophe brought on by collapsing land prices, rising interest rates, unsustainable farm debt,
and drought—for a distinctly rural identity to form. Only in
the past decade or so has a nationalized sense of ruralness
emerged where rural folks living in very different parts of the
country understood themselves as "a distinctive people."[13]
That rural distinctiveness is at least partly the product of divisive and sometimes politically expedient pressures. In seeking
to understand rural culture, we give credence to a divide that's
not always good or helpful. We have to tread carefully.

Because the contemporary rural church movement was also
born out of these cultural trends, those of us who spend time
thinking and writing about the rural church can all too easily
fall into the trap of over-defining rural. The philosophical term
for it is *reifying*, from the Latin *res* for "thing." We risk reifying rural, making it more of a thing than it really is and thus
accentuating the cultural divide. It's as if after years of saying
too little, we say too much. And that's a misunderstanding all
its own.

However we choose to understand rural, the point is not to slot people into our categories, but to see and hear and know them. Rural people are just people, and in asking the question *Where am I?*, we're not so much seeking to research rural people as if we were colonial anthropologists as we're seeking to become neighbors.

WHAT AM I DOING HERE?

"What are you teaching tomorrow?" my wife asked as I came home from preparing my adult Sunday school lesson.

When I told her, she nodded and asked, "So are you making it up, or using some other materials?"

"Oh, *amor mio*," I said. "I'm always making it up."

Of course, in the ways that matter most, I'm not making up anything that I preach or teach. I'm a scribe trained for the kingdom of heaven, nothing more.[14] My greatest aspiration is to bring "treasures old and new" from the abundant larder that the King left for his people. It was the Teacher who stared down the *tohu vabohu*, that formless void, and created. I'm just cobbling together something from his bright materials. In my view, it's a mark of pride to cling tenaciously to the faith "once for all entrusted to the saints" (Jude 3). An Orthodox priest once told me that when the coronavirus pandemic struck, his bishop contacted him with a warning: "Don't do anything creative." I like that. The ancient story and rites and Scriptures will carry us through.

Yet ministry is creative. We're laboring in an environment frothing with TV and sports and devices, devices, devices. Skilled pastors and leaders have to know their audience and work the angles that God grants them. Our society's sacred/profane toggle switch seems stuck somewhere staticky in the middle: we're all spiritual but not quite religious enough to wake up and string twenty steps together to the car for church.

And all the while we pastors and leaders are doing our own work. It's yeoman's work, oarsman's work in which we strain our backs against the current. Each week I lower the nets into the same dark waters as always, first one side and then the other, fishing for a fresh way to proclaim the ancient and ever-new gospel. I'm amazed every Sunday that I haven't run out of things to say. Chalk it up to the obvious richness of the Scriptures and the Spirit who teaches us everything and reminds us, at just the right time, of Jesus' words.

But there's something more. Creative, generative ministry involves constantly going back to basics and beginning again. We go back to the trunk, to the True Vine, to the only foundation that anyone can lay (John 15:1; 1 Corinthians 3:11). Jesus said that without him we can do nothing (John 15:5). He said he'll be with us always, even unto the end of the age (Matthew 28:20). Jesus didn't just mean that he would inspire us, like Confucius inspires Confucians, Mohammed inspires Muslims, or George Washington inspires young cherry tree cutters. Jesus meant that he would continue to work through us. He would minister in us for the life of the world. We're a kingdom of priests because the King and Priest is present among us as a soul in a body (1 Peter 2:9; Hebrews 4:14). Jesus may have ascended to the right hand of the Father, but by the Spirit he continues his ministry forever through the church. Jesus is, in fact, the one who is making it up as he goes along—and he's doing it through us.

I aspire to be a beginner. Not a know-nothing beginner, a careless dilettante who can't be bothered to parse Greek verbs, but a beginner with a teachable spirit, someone who is constantly going back to the beginning expecting that Jesus still shows up, that it is Jesus who brings what we need to the table in any given situation. The heart of ministry—and I think this is especially true of rural ministry—is becoming a coworker with Christ (1 Corinthians 3:9). "This is the secret for sustainable pastoral work," writes author and spiritual care expert Harold Senkbeil. "You need to realize that you've got nothing to give to others that you yourself did not receive."[15] And to our astonishment, we continue to receive it. Like generals, ministers are always fighting the last war. We have faith in the *last* rescue, the *last* time Jesus gave us the words, the last time his power improbably erupted in a life for healing. Somehow, we get surprised when Jesus shows up yet again, pushes open the door, and does his thing.

The disciples had the same struggle. They saw Jesus feed those five thousand plus. And then there they were again, fish and bread in hand but not enough for those fresh four thousand. Now what? Jesus and Jesus and Jesus yet again.

I love the call stories of Peter and Andrew, James and John. Jesus met them while they were tending their nets and said, "Follow me and I will make you fish for people" (Mark 1:17). The other gospel accounts tell us that a longer story took place before this seemingly radical call. Jesus had stayed at Peter's house (Luke 4:38–40). He had preached from Peter's boat. The Carpenter gave the fishermen pelagic instructions (Luke 5). After witnessing all of that, Peter, James, and John made the same decision as the guy who discovered a treasure buried in the field: they sold everything (or as it were: left everything) to follow Jesus (Matthew 13:44). And at the end of the gospel of John, after the death and resurrection of the beloved Son, there they were all over again: fishing those waters again, nets empty again, all that work for nothing again until the risen Lord, cloaked in mystery after his far journey to eternity and back, called to them from the shore, "Cast the net to the right side of the boat." The disciple whom Jesus loved exclaimed, "It is the Lord!" (John 21:6–7). And indeed it was: the Lord doing his *thing*, thy kingdom coming, already laboring in the new-birthed resurrection reality.

The disciples forgot. We all do. We forget that it is the Lord, the One who fills empty nets and takes, blesses, breaks, and gives bread by the 416 dozen. We're coworkers with Christ, our honed skills and heaps of degrees given their supernatural umph because he is working in and through them, through us (Ephesians 3:20–21; Philippians 2:13; Hebrews 13:21).

The late, great pastor and theologian Eugene Peterson wrote of the "organic continuities between Jesus and his company of followers." Says Peterson: "The more we get involved in what God is doing, the less we find ourselves running things; the more we participate in God's work revealed in Jesus, the more is done to us and the more is done through us."[16] We are stewards of mysteries that are not our own (1 Corinthians 4:1).

Once I did a mission trip to Mexico with a small group of leaders from the Pacific Northwest. We wove our way between the cities of Sinaloa and Sonora, visiting churches and encouraging local pastors. After an evening preaching and teaching in a small rural congregation, I found myself hunkered down in the back of a pickup truck with a handful of believers as we trundled back toward the city. Dust clouded up from the tires. The star-glossed sky was distant and brittle and cold. "*Pastor*," a man leaned over and asked me in Spanish. "What does it take to be a pastor?"

There's a lot one can say in response to that question in the back of a pickup truck at night in Mexico. A three-year MDiv, maybe? Reading knowledge of Greek and Hebrew? An internal sense of call confirmed by the church through ordination?

Mercifully, he gave me a moment to think by adding to his question. "I'm asking," he said, "because I'm serving as the pastor of our little rural congregation. And I can't read."

So what does it take to do ministry faithfully and well? The degree and the credentials—even basic reading—are all tools of the trade. But at its heart, ministry is about making ourselves available to Christ as he ministers among us to his people and world. Ministry is not a task-based job but a presence-based one (if it can even properly be called a "job"—it's really more a way of life). And so what we're about as rural pastors and leaders is not simply cultivating a particular skill set, but an internal disposition for rural ministry—not unlike what the apostle Paul does in describing the bundle of virtues required of bishops and deacons in 1 Timothy 3. We're developing a way of life.

Nowhere is this more the case than in rural ministry, where loops of school, sports, work, family, friends, enemies, and frenemies are crocheted across time and space. Pastors and leaders have got to be in, with, and for the community—just like the church. Rural ministry is community ministry, and this reality gives rural ministry its distinctive shape and style. We celebrate graduations even when it's not our congregation's youth walking across the stage. We mourn our town's losses and work for the common good. We commit to the basic act of love that is choosing to live in a place, with a people, over the long term. It's solidarity over some theory of "big man" urban influence supposedly percolating out to the rural edges and dredges. Says small-town pastor Stephen Witmer: "If you're kind, invested, and involved, you can become a pastor of a community."[17]

FROM THE BEGINNING

The gospel of Mark launches with these words: "The beginning of the good news of Jesus Christ, the Son of God" (Mark 1:1).

The next verse is a word from the ancient prophets. Then John rumbles in from the desert with honey on his beard and prophecy dripping from his lips. Prepare the way of the Lord! And he does prepare it, baptizing with water just as the one coming after him will baptize with the Holy Spirit (Mark 1:5–8).

When Jesus comes on the scene, he slides beneath Jordan's muddy waters in solidarity with sinful humanity (Mark 1:9–10). Thus begins his ministry: "The beginning of the good news of Jesus Christ." Temptation, healing, preaching, casting out demons, building the kingdom by his death and resurrection will follow. But first: prepare the way of the Lord, enter the waters, claim his identity as the Beloved. That's the beginning.

Except that it isn't really the beginning. Jesus came as Prophet, Priest, and King because the stage had been set by Isaiah and Melchizedek and David—and the ten thousand other prophets, priests, and kings who came before him. The great story of God's people had been unfolding for millennia to that moment. Simeon held the infant Christ in his arms (Luke 2:28). Anna blessed him (v. 38). Before Jesus overturned the tables in the temple, he came as a curious child to listen and ask questions in his Father's house (v. 46; Mark 11:15–17).

Thus it is for rural pastors and leaders. With Jesus as our model, we step into the wonderful particularity of the place to which God has called us and come to value place and people as we find them. Rural life—just as urban and suburban—possesses its own genius that we are invited to attend to and love. We minister from place to place. Rural pastors and leaders come into a place rich with stories and relationships. We learn to respect and value the narrative watershed of the community. This is not just because rural places know and define themselves by their stories and relationships, and therefore we can do no other, but because God was already at work before we came on the scene, unfolding the great story of God's love for this particular people and place. Thus it won't be so much by our expertise and smarts that we'll get where God needs us to go, but by a humble vulnerability that is willing to be present in a place and transparent to Christ working through us. We show up and we stay put.

Showing up and staying put might seem to set a rather low bar, were it not for two factors. First, too many pastors and leaders dismiss rural as second-rate, a poor return on their considerable investment of blood and treasure in pursuing a seminary education. Again and again, pastors have chosen not to show up in rural churches. (For that matter, many rural folks raised and lovingly discipled in small rural congregations effectively do the same thing—hitting the highway on Sunday morning—or claiming to, at least—for the big city church with its high production values.) Second, pastors often treat rural congregations as places to begin their ministry, but not to stay put and sweat and struggle. They move on to larger suburban or urban congregations after topping up their résumés in the sticks. Only recently, a community member volunteered that I should be working in a larger place so that I could influence more people with my wisdom. I wasn't sure if I should respond with "Aw shucks" or "Get behind me, Satan!"

Showing up and staying put are the beginning points of rural ministry, not its sum. They're the basic gifts of love that we give a people and a place, what make us available to Christ's ministering action.

Ministry advice often comes packaged as a how-to guide: Ten Steps to Make Your Church Grow. (Guaranteed!) This book is not that. If you've been helped by those sorts of books, I'm grateful. But when I've read them, they have struck me as overly strategic and confident and smug. Their ten steps have little to say to God's tiniest, beloved *middle-of-somewhere* places flung wide across this continent's dizzying expanse. When they purport to speak to rural at all, most of them turn out to be geared to small towns or even suburbs. Once I was at a conference where the speaker got up to address the assembled rural pastors and leaders and said, "I've never been to an event like this where everybody is bragging about how small their town is!" There's a vast difference between communities of 150,000 and 15,000 and 1,500. I'm particularly interested in writing to pastors and leaders serving rural communities that come in under the 2,500 population threshold, places so often casually disdained as "flyover country" in our cultural cartography. I want to brag on those smallest places. If it's "flyover country," then I want to trumpet the church in those far-off lands, the "flyover church."

Don't get me wrong: I don't believe that loving on rural requires disparaging anywhere else. The important thing, the calling and compulsion that all of us carry as Jesus' people, is to be present and to be sent. Jesus "came to Galilee" (Mark 1:14). His feet and his heart and his hands and his whole self were present, the God who "fills all in all" (Ephesians 1:23) scandalously so very right there in that place, moving through that particular time: Galilee, circa 30 AD. The bulk of Jesus' earthly life was spent hidden in Nazareth with his family, doing small craftsman's work and eating what was set before him. That's how he calls us to begin: by being where we are, from city skylines to suburban greenscapes to a couple of houses clustered around a grain elevator. We start by being present to our place, wherever that is.

And Jesus came "proclaiming the good news of God." He shared a message of hope and pioneered the healing path of the kingdom. God sent him from Galilee to Galilee. Us too:

we're a sent people, driven by the Spirit to the ends of the earth, wherever those ends happen to be—maybe the end of the block. Rural is indeed one of the ends, but there are others. I start with rural, but my hope is that whatever your setting, rural can be a doorway into thinking about how you're present and how you're sent in your neighborhood.

For this book, I've interviewed rural pastors and leaders from across the continent—from the Yukon to Massachusetts—and spanning diverse theological traditions. They're savvy practitioners of rural and small-town ministry, and hearing their voices can help us take in the breadth, texture, and significance of rural ministry.

Alongside their insights, I seek to track Jesus' cues into rural and small church ministry. After all, "Whoever says, 'I abide in him,' ought to walk just as he walked" (1 John 2:6). By following the life of Jesus in Mark and weaving in stories from my own experience and that of others, we'll develop a disposition for ministry tailored for rural places. Jesus faced temptation in the wilderness, made disciples, listened and told stories, walked on water (though Peter didn't), took up his cross, experienced resurrection, and proclaimed good news everywhere. Each of these movements is an overture to a way of life with him. The Gospels aren't just history, they're discipleship manuals. And I think they're manuals for ministry, too, though not the how-to kind. The Gospels are more evocative and invitational than prescriptive, communicating not a body of information but a breath and warmth of encounter with Jesus, the Living One with nail-marked hands who accompanies his people still. Maybe they're an anti-manual in that way. I chose Mark because his gospel is a lean yet weighty dive into the life of Jesus and the Jesus way of life—and that's what I want this book to be.

To read Mark—or any of the Gospels—is to envision what it looks like for Jesus to live and labor through us. My aspiration is this: to go back to the beginning and point to the ways that we can reconfigure our lives to the creative, always-new ministry of Christ in his flyover church.

2

The Spirit Drove Him into the Wilderness

The Spirit immediately drove him out into the wilderness.
—Mark 1:12

It's Tuesday morning. Do you know where your pastor is?

There are three parts to the geography of my week. Tuesday afternoon through Thursday are the plains, the times when I do the stuff of ministry. I write, lead meetings, strategize, dream, read, reach out, and attend to the odds and ends of my pastoral portfolio. Friday through Sunday, I scale the mountain of worship, craft my sermon, prepare to teach, and finally perform the word and lead the congregation in the movements of worship. After the last hand is shaken and the doors of the church locked, the power goes out of me. I recoup in the afternoon. (A nap helps). I take Monday off to recollect myself, work the cramps out of my writing muscles, and catch up on projects around the house.

But Tuesday mornings are a challenge. Tuesday mornings are a wilderness creased with jagged valleys. The self-justifying pressure of the weekend triduum gives way with a snap, and more often than not I find myself stumbling into the abyss, half startled, wondering what in the world I'm doing here. There you have it: confessions of a small-town pastor. It's Tuesday morning, and I'm daydreaming about becoming a plumber.

In the sometimes hardness of rural ministry, we can find ourselves staring into the abyss, facing the same temptations Jesus did in the wilderness to require God to conform to our wishes, pursue self-aggrandizement, or give up. Just as Jesus faced those temptations, so too he shows us the way forward as he experiences the Holy Spirit's soul-shaping power. The Spirit propels him to seek *more* for God and simultaneously surrender his expectations and dreams to the Father's will by doing *less*.

ONCE MORE INTO THE ABYSS

I most often find myself leaning over the abyss on Tuesday mornings. The abyss is the soul-deep threat to meaning that lingers at life's edges. It lies right beneath our feet. The abyss is like death, but worse, because even death can be given meaning by ritual and memory, philosophy or faith. The abyss is the existential dread that French philosophical types contemplated around smoky café tables beneath the shadow of the Eiffel Tower.

The abyss is a dark line undulating through Western literature, at least as old as the Bible. Take Ecclesiastes, a book whose presence in the canon of Scripture is always jarring to rookie readers because of its acid edginess. Ecclesiastes cuts through our smug theologies like antiseptic. The book is traditionally ascribed to Solomon, writing as a bitter philosopher-king from the iron glare of old age and lost youth. The abyss haunts Solomon. He writes: "I took a good look at everything I'd done, looked at all the sweat and hard work. But when I looked, I saw nothing but smoke. Smoke and spitting into the wind. There was nothing to any of it. Nothing" (2:11 *The Message*).

Or take the writings of Ernest Hemingway, that bleak-eyed war reporter hunched over his metallic typewriter as he punched out spare, punctilious prose, heart forever stained by the blood of the Spanish Civil War. In Hemingway's story, it is the abyss that the older waiter tries to chase away with his clean, well-lighted place, the "nothing that he knew too well." "Some lived in it and never felt it," Hemingway reflects through the waiter's voice. "But he knew it all was nada y pues nada y pues nada."[1]

Or think of Emily Dickinson, dressed in white and haunting her family home in Amherst, Massachusetts, dashing poems in folios as death's losses linger at the door. In poem 599 she writes of pain that "covers the Abyss with Trance"—a pain "so utter" that it swallows up all substance.[2]

Or read the poetry of Weldon Kees, that forgotten native son of the Great Plains. He wrote these gleefully biting lines: "Let's go down into the abyss. It won't be a really *awful* abyss: there'll be a lot of charming & good things in it: just no poets, that's all."[3] Of course, with no poets we're hopelessly lost in the abyss, swallowed up whole.

We all face the abyss in a deeply personal way as we strive to give meaning to our daily lives. It's the question of *What matters? Will my work endure?* Or simply: *Why get up in the morning?* We seek purpose in something larger, like family, faith, or nation. We throw ourselves into a personal mission, pour out our hearts in pursuit of a life that matters. We eat, sleep, and breathe *something*, and that something becomes our little candle against the darkness.

But the abyss can also be faced by whole communities—by towns, cities, and nations. We sense that there must be some deeper reason for the body politic to exist, a meaning that rises above the shuffling polis. *Liberté, égalité, fraternité* for some. Or the pursuit of happiness. Or God himself imbuing the nation with sacred purpose. A well-run bureaucracy won't do. We long for mythical dimensions.

So too, great cities have their own potent ways of facing the abyss. There's a sense of progress and action. There are universities and industries and gold-domed capitols with marble floors. The bustle of the city gives people a sense of purpose. If nothing else, there's professional sports. We can all find our identity in that. And if the meaning we find is sometimes superficial, well, at least in the city it's got a big, thumping heart underneath. Something about the way the horizons of the city go up makes us feel strong and important, like the poet Carl Sandburg rhapsodizing Chicago, that "tall, bold slugger."[4] The city's piston-crank and cocksure smokestacks give off a comforting hum. With all that jazz, we forget ourselves. Abyss? What abyss?

It's different in rural communities.[5] Rural communities are thin places for the abyss. Many of the towns dotting the Great Plains were founded as water stops along the old train routes, at least according to legend. Now that the train's just passing through, that old purpose is all dried up. As a reporter from a big Midwestern city once said to me, "There's really no reason for a lot of these communities to exist." Many people in the nation's smallest communities have come to the same conclusion, voting with their feet in places like Jewell County, Kansas, which lost half of its population between 1970 and 2000.[6]

Thus for many rural communities in America, the question is not simply *why* they should exist, but *whether* they should exist. Rural communities have to defend and contend for their very existence. No one questions the purpose of Washington, DC. It just is. But Washington, Kansas? Where's that, and why hasn't everyone moved to Kansas City?

Like it or not, rural pastors and leaders choke on the same smoke rising from the abyss. It's not so much that we feel we deserve more or better, that rural places are somehow beneath us (three years of graduate study for this?). The pull of the abyss is much more subtle than that. Its effects are all too obvious yet difficult to clearly see. We can become defensive about our role and claims to success. It's a common trope among rural pastors (or at least: speakers at rural pastor conferences) to point out that the hundred people who attend their church represent such-and-such large percent of the population of their community. Imagine that umpteen percent of Boston or Kansas City or Dallas attending your church. Eat your heart out, Big City Pastor!

Or not.

This sort of counting is just one more variation on trying to nail down meaning by measuring it in the usual ways: How many and how much? It's extent as a stand-in for significance. What's the breadth and length and height and depth of your church and influence?

But the rural church and rural community will scarcely measure up by those lights, and society and the broader church will conspire to favor the urbs and suburbs where Something's Really Happening. The abyss yawns under our feet, and we become hurried and frantic in our drive to shape things up, right the ship, light a fire. Or we realize (often after said hurried and frantic stage) that it ain't going to happen—at least not like it did for the guy on the big stage—and we grow disappointed.

I confess that I've fallen into both temptations: hurry and disappointment. Hurry is my usual habit—and my kryptonite.

I need the Scriptures to warn me off. Proverbs 19:2: "One who moves too hurriedly misses the way." In ministry we can confuse hurry with the drive to diligence. Diligence is vital: Think, plan, engage. Do the work. Excel in your giftings, not least by pushing forward as a "leader, in diligence" (Romans 12:8). This is my *thing*. I aspire to diligence—at least on my better days. I read up, plan ahead, come prepared.

Yet aspiring to diligence can have the unfortunate co-symptom of hurry, and hurry is often the ringleader for anxiety, carelessness, and vainglorious self-centeredness—that rangy goblin band. In hurrying along our way, we overlook what matters most. We might even miss the way.

Our hurry is often sponsored by implicit spiritual assumptions, including the belief that by hurrying through certain stretches of life (or maybe all of life), we'll arrive at the actual life we desire. But this is the "vanity of vanities," a misattribution of how we achieve wisdom, knowledge, and joy (Ecclesiastes 1:2; 2:26). In an ultimate sense, hurry won't get us where we need to go. It's the Lord who "builds the house" (Psalm 127:1).

In rural communities, hurry may also cause us to miss opportunities to connect. In his book *Small Town Jesus*, pastor Donnie Griggs writes of the importance of taking the time for small talk and chance encounters. "Always acting like you have somewhere better to be will eventually lead you to unnecessarily offending [people] in small towns," Griggs says.[7] What's more, leaders in a hurry can harm the church. Hurry torques process. It introduces anxiety and suspicion. People think: *Why the rush? Maybe we should drag our feet until we know where this is going.* Hurry can lead to burnout for leaders and congregations, along with other, more insidious spiritual harms. As monk and eventual saint Benedict of Nursia warned in the sixth century, if the leader over-drives the flock, they will "all die in one day."[8] This goes for the over-driven shepherd too. Writes Benedict: "Such a man is never at rest."

It seems to me that there's a place for engaged diligence that is not afraid to move quickly and work hard. And there's a place for luxurious presence-keeping, practicing the art of unhurriedly being with others—and with God. It's not always easy to know which is called for at any given moment. Wisdom is required.

The second risk—and this one has a distinctly rural edge—is disappointment. It's all too easy to become disappointed with the state of the church, with the community the church is located in, with (when we dare admit it) ourselves. Sometimes, this disappointment can take a devious form: seemingly innocent daydreaming about what we're missing out on, where we might—with all our degrees and supposed skills—accomplish more. Disappointment gives the illusion of being a neutral judgment. And, yes, at times disappointment can be generative because it can prompt us to try to change things. It can catapult us to greatness. But more often than not in the rural church, the root of disappointment is just pride.

On the contrary, the path to spiritual maturity runs through a humility that accepts people and place and our life with them as they come. There's a kind of grace in that, in just *being with* and not passing the implicit judgment of disappointment.

Toward the end of my tenure in my first congregation, I was caught up short when a leader in our congregation said with no rancor or irony, "I'm sorry our church hasn't been what you hoped." She was gentle and sincere, but it was a glass of cold prophetic water to the face. In all my striving to move the church onto a growth path, to foreground mission, to preach the word in season and out, to shepherd the people—in all of that I had failed in loving the congregation and the community as I found it. I had become disappointed—that the church wasn't growing like it should have, that the community wasn't responding to my obvious gifts, that my furious experimentation in all things strategic hadn't paid off. My disappointment was an oozing ulcer. Her words hurt, but with the good pain of truth striking home. Suddenly, I saw a new panorama. Everything the light touches is God's kingdom.

Eugene Peterson interprets the biblical story of Jonah as a parable of vocation and ministry. Jonah "had reduced his vocation to his own performance—being in the right place, doing the right thing—but he interpreted everything through his Jonah ideas, his Jonah desires." I saw myself as a type of Jonah in that church member's words. I had stomped through the center of town and plopped down under the kikayon plant. So many of us have been there: "disappointed and quarrelsome that our procedures result in something quite different from what we had anticipated."[9] But the kikayon casts its shade over the abyss.

ENTER THE WILDERNESS

Jesus confronted the abyss with its temptations to hurry and disappointment by entering the wilderness. In fact, the wilderness was the abyss, and Jesus entered it and passed through it in order to conquer it.

Wilderness has a double meaning in the Scriptures. It's a place of struggle and refuge, of encounter with God and withdrawal from the wiles of society. God calls his people out of Egypt to worship him in the desert wilderness (Exodus 3:18). They celebrate the Passover in the wilderness and receive the Law in the wilderness (Numbers 9; Exodus 19:1). In the Scriptures, the journey through the wilderness is portrayed as a journey toward God. And yet the wilderness is dangerous, a place of snakes and thirst and hunger (Deuteronomy 8:15–16). It's in the wilderness that the people of Israel know scarcity and vulnerability (Exodus 16:3; Deuteronomy 1:27). But it's also in the wilderness that the cloud of God's presence leads the people and where God feeds them on the bread of angels (Numbers 10:12; Psalm 78:25). In the symbolic language of the book of Revelation, the "woman clothed with the sun" (that is, Israel/Mary/the church) escapes the devil by taking refuge in the wilderness (Revelation 12:1, 14). That's where Jesus goes: into this double-sided wilderness.

Mark makes a spare rendition of the gospel narrative of the wilderness temptation: "[Jesus] was in the wilderness forty days, tempted by Satan; and he was with the wild beasts; and the angels waited on him" (Mark 1:13). Luke and Matthew tug at the story's accordion edges, and we see the devil in his wicked subtle glory, flinging sidewinder questions at the Son of Man (chapter 4 in both gospels). Turn those stones into loaves. *A man's gotta eat.* Take a flying leap. *His angels won't let you dash your precious foot against a stone.* Send one teensy word of praise my way. *And all these voluptuous nations will be yours. No nails, no cross, only crowns, crowns, crowns!* Jesus met the triple abyss of requiring God to conform to his wishes, pursuing self-aggrandizement, or giving up. And he said no, no, and no.

Jesus faced down the devil at the beginning of his ministry, but it wasn't the last battle. Luke tells us that the devil "departed from him until an opportune time" (4:13). There's at least one further moment in the Gospels when the devil's attack comes into plain view: at Caesarea Philippi, just after Peter's triumphal declaration that Jesus was the Christ (Mark 8:29). Indeed he was, and the Christ would have to suffer, would be rejected, would be killed—and would rise. Peter had gotten the right answer once, so he tried again. But his attempt at correcting Jesus' theology by insisting that the Messiah not suffer and die didn't get any traction with the Son of Man. Jesus caught him up short: "Get behind me, Satan! For you are setting your mind not on divine things but on human things" (Mark 8:31–33).

There won't be any single turning point in our lives when we struggle our way out of the abyss or—like Jonah—get coughed up out of it, bleached and steaming. If the highways to Zion are inscribed on our hearts, then they run always through the wilderness.[10] The wilderness is clingy and insistent and all too portable. We carry it within us.

Which means that we'll face the abyss again and again— maybe every Tuesday morning. We'll be tempted to create grand plans and demand that God get on board. We'll build it and demand that they come. We'll pep our people through meetings, pep them in sermons, pep ourselves up with CAFFEINE!

Good luck. As prayer writer Pete Grieg puts it, "Intensity and earnestness rarely attract the Holy Spirit."[11]

Others of us will make it about ourselves, pushing off of our congregation's foibles and shallow growth curve to aggrandize ourselves: all we've done, all we've tried, all our smart, smart strategies. This line into the abyss usually leads through the exit door. We're off to greener pastures! Except the same hungry souls are still living in the same little rural place after we've hit the road, and our own soul still pants within us.

Or we give up and move on. True, sometimes giving up and moving on is the right thing to do. Vocation is not coterminous with ministry position. But is career change sometimes a failure of nerve?

The disappointments of rural ministry can ring all too true: limited opportunities for outreach, a potent culture of stability that can tend toward immobility, social cohesion to the point of xenophobia. These are the wilderness's wild beasts (Mark 1:13). And they're not just a figment of our perceptions. It's the wilderness, after all.

While all of these things may be true, I'm convinced that each of them can be addressed or overcome, and that none of them on their own lead to the abyss. At root, we face the abyss because of one question, the question that all of us ask about our lives at some point or another: Am I making a difference? Writes Stephen Witmer: "I want to know that what I'm doing counts. I want to know deep in my bones that it's not a waste for me to minister on the periphery in this small, unknown town rather than in the center of things in a great city."[12]

But how, exactly, can we know we're making a difference?

MAGIS AND GELASSENHEIT

Here are two ways: doing more and doing less. I want to draw on two ancient concepts from two very different theological traditions: the Jesuit concept of the *magis*—the *more*—and the Anabaptist commitment to *Gelassenheit*—yieldedness to God's will.

Jesuits speak of the *magis* as the special genius of the teaching of Ignatius of Loyola. Ignatius, the founder of the Jesuit order, was a fifteenth-century soldier, dueler, womanizer, and all-around hothead who earned himself an extended retreat at a Spanish Catholic hospital after losing an argument with a cannonball. With all those crucifixes gazing down on him and little to read but the lives of the saints, Ignatius found himself vulnerable to God's grace in a new way. The experience provoked him to rethink his life. What was success? What was happiness? How should he live? The key question Ignatius meditated on, and the one that he would later teach as part of his celebrated *Spiritual Exercises*, was this: *What more can I do for the love of Jesus?* He didn't mean what more could he do to *earn* the love of Jesus. That love comes by grace. Ignatius was asking what more he could do *in response* to the love of Jesus. He had stumbled into the great driver of all Christian zeal and accomplishment. As Paul puts it in 2 Corinthians: "The love of Christ urges us on" (2 Corinthians 5:14). Ignatius saw this love pouring forth in an outward manifestation of *more*, a holy ambition that compelled him to found the Jesuit order—an order that would rise to fame for its fearless missionary work around the world and founding of universities. Ignatius invites us to seek "that which is more to the glory of the Divine Majesty and the salvation of my soul."[13]

Ignatius was rediscovering what the apostles knew first-hand. When Peter stood on that seashore by that campfire after Jesus' resurrection, dripping from his half-awkward dive into the sea to reach his Lord and teacher, Jesus put the question to him: "Do you love me more than these?" (John 21:15). Peter had already demonstrated a superhuman capacity to serve his Lord when, at Jesus' bidding, Peter did what all the disciples together could not manage: single-handedly drawing ashore the nets with their 153 fish.[14] It was a Spirit-pumped feat of strength, a *more* not unlike the gospel drive that would later send Peter out on the road to spread the good news and lead him to Rome and upside-down martyrdom. Peter loved Jesus *more*.

If we're going to contend with all the limitations of the wilderness, we need a *magis*-geared approach. We need *more*. It's not a strategy. The *magis* isn't any one thing. It's an approach to the wilderness that sees possibility and potential, that is willing to struggle, to strive, to try. *More* means seeing not just lack, but also potential. It's a holy hunger to attempt something big for Christ, even in—perhaps especially in!—small places. If the wild beasts dwell in the wilderness, those chupacabras of hurry and disappointment and disillusionment, then so too the angels wait on us. We're in the wilderness because the Spirit called (drove!) us there. We have been named beloved. We have gifts and graces. Jesus uses humble instruments—us crackpots—to show forth his strength and carry out his ministry, and because of that we can do *more*.[15]

Magis presents risks. Experts in Jesuit spirituality acknowledge that *magis* can lead to a caffeinated focus on doing in which we go, go, go until we can't go anymore—not just *more*, but *too much*. Certain types of personalities are particularly at risk for this.[16] Leaders can become overextended, get burned out. And congregations—especially small and aging ones—need to squarely face issues of sustainability. "Let's do more!" has been the rallying cry of a thousand fledgling pastors—and too many eulogies for their spent congregations. Further, in striving for more we pastors can sometimes fail to take seriously the ways that God has been at work among a people before we showed up. We can fail to treat the congregation as the Lord's beloved work in progress.

Yet while Jesus called Peter to love him *more*, so too Jesus taught, "Apart from me you can do nothing" (John 15:5). Peter may have hauled the catch of fish in by himself, but the nets were full only because of Jesus. The manna coated the wilderness ground because God opened the heavens. All is grace.

Which is why rural pastors and leaders must also learn to do *less* for Christ. I see doing less for Christ embodied in the beloved Anabaptist spiritual quality of *Gelassenheit*. *Gelassenheit* is a posture of yieldedness to God in all things. It's Anabaptism's little treasure, borne through fire and water from the sixteenth century. *Gelassenheit* is an approach to

taking up our cross and following Jesus every day. Historically, *Gelassenheit* has been translated into concrete forms of
yieldedness to God in self-defense and possession.

To do less for Christ is to recognize that our ministry is not
merely a product of our own efforts.[17] It's not all up to us to
make something happen. The church is a supernatural reality,
forged along divine-human lines as we take up our calling as
fellow workers with God (1 Corinthians 3:9). It turns out that
we have to do what the bumper stickers have been telling us
all along: Let go and let God.

There are practical reasons for this, not least a recognition
that what the church needs most is beyond our capacity to
produce—because of the limitations of congregational dynam-
ics and limits to our leadership abilities, but also because of the
deep mystery that is God's providence. *Less* for Christ means
recognizing that though we may struggle all night on the sea,
it is God who fills the nets.

One of the main reasons I accepted the call to eastern
Washington State after graduating from seminary was because
of the congregation's surrounding multicultural community.
Spanish-speaking folks, mainly from Mexico, had arrived in
waves over the previous fifty years. This little rural church
boasted a number of members who had done service and
mission in Latin America, knew Spanish, and cared about
reaching out. The church already hosted a Spanish-speaking
congregation in their building. My wife and I spoke Spanish.
I had done my ministry internship in a Spanish-speaking congregation in Indiana. "It sounds like a really good fit for you,"
said a student colleague as we edged toward graduation and
traded plans. "I know," I said. A perfect fit.

I hit the ground running in the fall, going through the usual
stumbles and spates of being utterly perplexed that every

first-call pastor experiences (a sermon *every* week!). And then one dark night in the desert winter, the phone rang. It was the pastor of the Spanish-speaking congregation. "Buenas noches," he said. The rest of the conversation has gone blurry in my memory, but the long and the short of it was: "We're going back to Argentina. Good luck."

At that point, I tried to do too much and fix problems that weren't mine to fix. I made a lot of mistakes and had to grow through some pretty trying stuff. But one of most challenging aspects was my sense that the whole reason I was there was to do cross-cultural ministry, and now that little church was falling apart. My sense of calling and my sense of identity were wrapped up in going out there to do that *thing*, my *thing*, what I had been called to, and suddenly I wasn't sure I was going to be able to do any of it.

And yet God was at work in more ways that I knew. He used my gifts in ways I could not have anticipated, and he led me to grow through that time in ways I would never have chosen for myself.

Looking back, it was a moment ripe for *Gelassenheit*. I should have listened more and spoken less. I should have sat with ambiguity more and resolved things less. I should have let things be what they were and strategized less. That little congregation faced a situation of profound uncertainty, and because I had a dream for myself that required them, I sought to fix it. I couldn't.

It's all too easy to get *magis* and *Gelassenheit* wrong, to fall into what Dwight Sandoz, an Assemblies of God pastor who teaches in the rural ministry program at Trinity Bible College and Graduate School in Ellendale, North Dakota, calls the "two ruts of rural ministry"—doing too much or doing too little.[18] In my experience, the risk of doing too much is greater than the risk of doing too little. We're wired, by training and culture, to do something. Don't just stand there. Pastors are often inveterate fixers. We want to help. To stand by, to wait, to be present and allow a situation to just be in all its knotty unfixableness would seem a dereliction of duty. Yet doing less and allowing things to be as they are is often precisely what God's calling us to. Even in the pressing work of tackling systemic injustice in our rural communities, the first step is to be present, to learn to know, to love.[19]

Doing less is especially key when we think about church size. More often than not, we pastors see the small size of our congregations as a problem to tackle, one that we could fix if only we and (especially) the congregation would just try a little harder, get a little more on our A-game. But there are deep risks in this approach, not least that we may sometimes be "fighting against God" (Acts 5:39). As small-church guru Karl Vaters writes, "What if by trying to fix a problem that isn't a problem, we're actually working against a strategy that God wants us to enact?"[20] This is where we need yieldedness to the greater purposes of God. This is where we need to learn to do less.

The catalytic power of these opposing poles of *more* and *less* is that they are not in fact opposites. *Magis* and *Gelassenheit* are so much more tricksome and elusive and compelling than that. We practice both at once, or we practice neither truly.

Ultimately, to enter the wilderness and face the abyss involves an openness to allowing Christ to work in and through us. It means avoiding the expectations trap, whether those expectations are imposed by our culture, by other leaders, or by our own wayward hearts with their longings for approval and acclaim and success. Instead we choose—as Jesus did—to live by every word, whether more or less, that comes from the mouth of God (Matthew 4:4).

3

Proclamation and Calling Disciples

Jesus came to Galilee, proclaiming the good news of God, and saying, "The time is fulfilled, and the kingdom of God has come near; repent, and believe in the good news." —Mark 1:14–15

It was Saturday morning in Seattle, and my wife and I were taking a break from ministry to explore Pike's Place Market downtown. It was sometime early in my first call. We had journeyed over the mountains, left our kids with friends, and made our way down to the pier. Pike's Place is a standard tourist destination, a sprawling market famous for good coffee, local art, and fishmongers tossing fish.

We came out of the upper level of the market, and in between the watercolors of the Pacific Northwest, bundles of tulips, and touristy trinkets were evangelists: The End Is Near sandwich board guys, street preacher guys, guys with pamphlets. We stepped into the chill air and took in the sweep of the humped horizon of the Olympic Mountains and the lush gray-blue of Puget Sound. That's when a big guy approached us. He asked bluntly: "Have you accepted Jesus Christ as your personal Lord and Savior?"

This was in my Earnest Young Pastor Period, and I wore a small bronze cross around my neck at all waking hours. Just then, that cross was hidden beneath a down vest. "I have!" I responded, unzipping my vest and pulling it back to reveal the cross like some kind of Superman. "And not only that, I'm a pastor!"

Big Guy looked me up and down, considering me for a long moment. Then in a low growl he said: "You better be."

I've only encountered real, honest-to-goodness evangelists a handful of times in my life. There was a guy at a big city workout park, hitting people up for Jesus while they tried to get in their pull-ups. There was that street preacher outside the museum. There was this man at Pike's Place. And while I admire their pluck and determination in sharing the gospel, I'm not always sure about their methods. They make me a little nervous.

Of course, *a* method is better than *no* method.

If Jesus had an evangelistic method, it was woven into the fabric of his life. Sure, at the beginning he made a splash. Mark tells us that after Jesus returned from the desert, he came to his home district of Galilee "proclaiming the good news of God." The kingdom is near! "Repent, and believe in the good news" (Mark 1:14–15). But then Jesus does the most human and basic and uncaffeinated thing: he encounters people, builds relationships, and speaks the good news. And he does it all with a perfectly uncalculated authenticity. Jesus also happened to do these things in rural places, and his method fits rural places.

I love talking to people about Jesus, but I'm a terrible evangelist. A few years ago, God laid on my heart that the work he's calling me to do is threefold: pray, write, and evangelize.

I've got the first two down pat. I flub the last one more often than I might care to admit.

I plopped into a corner of our coffee shop one afternoon with a laptop and warm cup of joe. I'm a classic introvert, so working in a public area is always a little iffy for me—more "working" than working. But I wanted to get out of the office and position myself to be with people. Mine was an evangelistic move.

As I sipped at my coffee, I noticed a couple of folks across the room whom I didn't recognize. In rural communities, you start to get to know the regulars. You bump into people. You see them around. Unfamiliar faces often mean new people, and these folks were unfamiliar to me. When they struck up a conversation with the barista at the counter, my ears perked up. "We're not from here," one of them said. "And we're wondering if there's anything going on this weekend?"

I started praying. I threw out my fleece, asking the Lord to open a door for me to talk to them if it was his will. I got up and walked past them to return my mug. I paused. I turned and walked past them again.

And I left. I didn't talk to them. I didn't invite them to our special outreach service and meal we were doing *that Sunday*. I was too—what?—(shy)(second-guessing)(doubting), scared. It's not always like that for me. But sometimes, it is. As I said: a terrible evangelist.

Part of my challenge in evangelism, the part that I fear, is coming off as fake. Sure, starting a conversation around ultimate beliefs and values with perfect strangers is difficult for me. But more than anything, I don't want to come off as *that* guy, that plastic preacher, that evangelist who knows not a thing about another's life but is ready to upsell the gospel.

Jesus began his public ministry with proclamation, and he called his first disciples to proclaim the good news of the kingdom. "Follow me," said Jesus, "and I will make you fish for people." To follow Jesus is to share the gospel with others. To become a disciple is to make more disciples. The apostle Paul got this. What you have heard from me, he told Timothy, "entrust to faithful people who will be able to teach others as well" (2 Timothy 2:2). Writes pastor David Platt: "Every disciple of Jesus exists to make disciples of Jesus. . . . There are no spectators."[1] Evangelism isn't an evangelical thing. Disciple-making isn't a charismatic thing or a Baptist thing or a church plant thing. It's a Jesus thing. Everybody who follows Jesus learns the art of people-angling.

What I've discovered is that evangelism and disciple-making play out in distinct ways in rural communities. A frantic, caffeinated agenda to grab people and drag them into church won't work. Like Jesus, we have to go to where people are and spend time with them, building relationships. Jesus demonstrates three key practices in the gospels: we connect, we speak, and we do it with authenticity. All of this presumes that we go out, that we have a hunger to make disciples, and that we're willing to be made fools for Christ (or at least be made uncomfortable for Christ) in order to share the gospel with others.

THE LURE OF STRATEGY

Evangelism in the modern era has long been at risk of falling into strategy and technique. At the turn of the nineteenth century, the revival movement that came to be known as the Second Great Awakening caught flame across the growing United States. Charley Finney, a Presbyterian lawyer-turned-evangelist who had recently experienced a religious conversion himself, began leading revival meetings in upstate New York.[2] Finney spoke of his "new measures" intended to spark a conversion experience. He employed a convicting style of preaching, coaxed people to sit in the "anxious bench," or prodded them to respond to altar calls.[3] I suppose that none of these things is bad in and of itself. I preach to convince, and we've done altar calls in my church. But what set Finney apart from earlier generations of leaders was his reliance on human strategy and technique to provoke conversion rather than waiting on the Spirit's providential timing. A lot of us on the North American scene—particularly in evangelical circles—have been relying on some form of our own "new measures" ever since.

And why not? The logic appears so sound: If we can do our work well and skillfully, design our worship services to pluck an exciting bass-thump nerve, pitch our messages to just the right register of meaning, then people will come. The results speak for themselves. The big churches, the fast churches, the growing churches are all doing these things—or at least, it would seem that way. I've witnessed it. A congregation in a nearby rural community hired a capable pastor to turn things around. Nothing. They built a gymnasium and sought to position themselves as a community church. No dice. But when they closed down, gave their assets to an expanding congregation in another town that redid the sanctuary, changed their name, and came back with a guitar-driven sound, things took off. Something there is about our age that does not love a pipe organ.

Still, in rural congregations, reliance on strategy and technique has an old and not-so-venerable history. In his 1922 book *Rural Church Life in the Middle West*, author Benson Landis approvingly quotes a "rural secretary of the home mission board of a large denomination." Declares said rural secretary in what can only be read in a 1920s radio voice: "We know that the country church is sick, very sick, but give us enough money and the right kind of men, and we will solve the problems."[4] (Oh yes, that's just as loaded as it sounds).

Here we are, a century later. I wonder whether Landis's home secretary would make the same diagnosis—or propose the same cure. I'm doubtful that strategy and technique will get us where we need to go at this moment in the rural church. What I'm convinced we need most is the ancient treasure of the gospel, the "what is new and what is old" of connecting and speaking and practicing authenticity (Matthew 13:52).

CONNECTING

Jesus was a carpenter. His labor was in a carpentry workshop with his father, Joseph. But he didn't launch his ministry from a back street of Nazareth. He went to the beach. "Jesus passed along the Sea of Galilee" (Mark 1:16). That's where the people were—or at least: the people he intended to connect with. They were the boat captains and the fishmongers and above all: the fishermen, those who knew the daily, persistent, sometimes fruitless work of casting their nets again and again into the waters. Jesus went to the people, and he connected with them.

If there are steps to rural evangelism, this is the first: connect. It's simple in one way, but in another way, connecting can be a dicey proposal. Connecting can be easy to get wrong, because we can come off as operating on a mercenary's calculus, more interested in getting somebody into church than in getting to know them. As a rule, I never invite people to church on the first encounter. This is a rule born of experience: I've gotten off on the wrong foot with people too many times, left looking like the only reason I bothered talking to them is because I want to get them into church.

Of course, rules are made to be broken. Not long ago, I met a new neighbor on the block when we crossed paths in the street. I introduced myself—not as the pastor of the church, just as the neighbor. I welcomed the family to our block. The neighbor introduced me to her kids. I talked about mine. That was it. We were about to go our separate ways when she asked, "What time is church?" And they came.

Jesus went out and connected with people. There aren't many words in Mark's gospel account. It's all very cut and dried and simple. Jesus just met them and said, "Follow me." As noted earlier, the gospel of Luke gives the impression that Peter and some of these other disciples already knew Jesus (see 4:38–44). Perhaps Jesus's encounter with them on the beach wasn't their first, but rather the next stage of an unfolding relationship.

I find it interesting that once Jesus went out to make disciples, he never went back. I mean, he did go home again. Much of his ministry was spent in Galilee. But as far as we know, he never went back to being a carpenter. I don't know, maybe he repaired the odd chair or two. A pastor from Mexico once stayed with us for a few days. His day job was as a carpenter, and he emerged from our basement guest room one morning asking for tools. The bed he was sleeping in had a cracked storage drawer, and he fixed it. Maybe it was like that with Jesus. He healed Peter's mother-in-law, cast out demons, "cured many who were sick with various diseases" lined up outside the door to Peter's house (Mark 1:33–34). And then planed and rehung the door. Who knows? But he never went back to his old life. Jesus was always about connecting. His way of life was discipleship.

Part of the genius of the early church was that it didn't train people in evangelistic technique. The early church formed what it called a *habitus* in them. Rooted in Aristotle's understanding of how virtue is fostered and lived out, habitus stands for a "kind of embodied tradition," a cluster of values and impulses that orders our lives and behaviors around Christ.[5] And this habitus was intensely yet patiently evangelistic. Writes scholar of early Christianity Alan Kreider: "Christian leaders didn't think or write about how to systematize the spread of Christianity; they were not concerned to cover the world evenly with evangelistic efforts. Instead the Christians concentrated on developing practices that contributed to a habitus that characterized both individual Christians and Christian communities. They believed that when the habitus was healthy, the churches would grow."[6]

And so it was. The gospel took off across the Roman Empire because apostles like Paul carried the word to new places, but also because believers took myriad quotidian opportunities to speak of their faith to those close to them. They connected with people.

This was Paul's way of doing things too. Imagine him in a rented room, tent canvas rumpled on the floor as he measures and cuts and sews and talks—to other tentmakers, to suppliers, to some errand slave boy who lingers at the door, to Aquila and Priscilla, those recent refugees from Claudius's purge of Rome's Jews (Acts 18:1–3). It wasn't any extra effort for Paul. It was just who he had become. His life had become oriented outward. Like Paul, those who took refuge in the church would go on to be formed in a habitus of connecting.

Connecting with people for the sake of the kingdom can seem heroic or strenuous, the kind of thing we might gear ourselves up for, blurt out our canned lines about Jesus saving them from their sins, turn red, and back away before they can ask too many questions. Author Ed Cyzewski writes about his experience studying in an evangelical seminary that placed a premium on sharing faith with others. He was urged to do it. He was trained to do it. He was sent out to do it. But the drive to evangelize gave him panic attacks—and it provoked something of a crisis of faith. The evangelism methods he was taught, writes Cyzewski, "made me completely unable to have normal conversations with people such as my car mechanic or the cashier at the supermarket."[7]

That doesn't feel like what Jesus modeled. Connecting seems like the most everyday, most non-jittery, unstrenuous thing for him. Jesus' style of evangelism looks precisely like having normal conversations with people.

Brandon Weddle, a young pastor in deeply rural Ten Sleep, Wyoming, told me that when he and his wife were newcomers to Ten Sleep, they aimed to attend every sporting event at the local school. They had quickly picked up on the fact that community life revolved around the school. So that's where they went, sitting in the bleachers with perfect strangers watching other people's kids play. Weddle said that they didn't invite people to church. They just connected. And their little Assemblies of God congregation began to grow, increasing from seventeen mostly older folks to some sixty people with a smattering of kids.[8]

Taking the time to connect with people is vital in rural communities because many people are already deeply connected. Roots run deep. People situate themselves in a matrix of friendships and rivalries, marriages and breakups. The fruit doesn't fall far from the tree—or it does—and pastors are often the last to know. And so we have to play it cool, be with people, take time to connect.

Connecting involves attentiveness to others, both in inter-personal relationships and as an approach to the community. We pay attention to what matters to us, so when we pay attention to people and community and take the time to learn what they care about, what they celebrate, what makes them tick, we're saying: *You matter to me.* We're quick to listen and slow to speak (James 1:19).

A Baptist church planter in small-town Utah told me how the seeds for the congregation he leads were planted in his day job as a house painter. Conversations happened in living rooms while he rolled out the wall. He listened to people. He honored the community and the values people had received from their Mormon faith tradition. When he eventually started a Bible study, he cast the invitation to join from a place of appreciation.

My city's municipal offices used to send me a list of every-one new who had moved to town. (Yes, I'm sure it was slightly sketchy, but I asked and they said yes.) My wife and I would knock on the door of their homes with a plate of cookies in hand and a church postcard taped to the bottom. Welcome to town! One young couple was ready to talk. I later realized that he mowed our neighbors' lawn, and I struck up a conversation with him again. Then we floated into each other at the public pool. Then we saw each other at the park for the summer com-munity celebration. And so on, until their kids sang in a chil-dren's choir we organized one winter and they started coming to church. Somewhere along the way, we learned that they weren't married. They asked, and I performed their wedding. We became their church, and I was their pastor. It all started with a knock on the door and a perfectly normal conversation from a perfectly straightforward connection.

SPEAKING

Francis of Assisi famously *didn't* say, "Preach the gospel at all times. Use words if necessary." My Mennonite people don't venerate saints, but we really like Saint Francis—or at least we like pop-Francis, the Jesus-hippie version who preached peace and was kind to animals. We mostly haven't heard of the Saint Francis of *Little Flowers* fame who preached repentance and warned of blasphemy and the fires of hell. But hey. Mennonites talk a lot about actions speaking louder than words, about showing rather than speaking the gospel. We like stories of people seeing us in gospel action, developing an attraction to our way of life, and wending their way to the Jesus who animates our lives.

It works, some of the time. A family in a church I served started attending because the dad admired one of our elder saints. "I want to be like him," he confided to me.

But most people aren't all that observant. They can't tell the difference between sacrificial kindness and just-doing-my-job niceness. Waitstaff are nice. Social workers are nice. The customer is always right in the big box return line. So unless you donate a kidney or rebuild their house after a tornado, most people most of the time won't notice your Jesus way of life.

It's not for lack of effort on our part; it's for lack of ears to hear. The world cannot receive the Spirit, "because it neither sees him nor knows him" (John 14:17). As far as the world is concerned, the church and everyone in it belong to a puzzling social club delivering buggy community service. Folks will never know that one church in town quietly began paying down overdue electric bills without seeking any recognition. They'll forget the blood drive and the thrift shop, the food pantry and the daycare. They'll be clueless about the church's greatest work and kindness: silent, constant, intercessory prayer on their behalf rising day after week after century.

In other words, a haloed lifestyle alone cuts no ice. At some point, we have to use words. We have to speak. That's what Jesus did. He went to people, and he talked to them. He said the kingdom of God is like seed scattered and sown. The seed is the word. The ground is people. The word has to be flung far and wide. It's true that the gospel is caught, not taught. But it's aerosolized by speaking.

Speaking can't mean sermonizing in our rural communities. I mean, I preach sermons all the time, nearly every Sunday, words and words and piles of words. And sermonizing evangelism may work for funerals and revival services. But it falls short most of the rest of the time. Sermons have a powerful declarative function, but what people need is not so much to be spoken to, but to be heard. "Always be ready to make your defense," says Peter, "to anyone who demands from you an accounting for the hope that is in you" (1 Peter 3:15). "Defense" sounds backfooted and, well, defensive. But what we miss is the subtext: Someone has asked us to explain our faith. Someone else asked. It means that previous conversation has led to this moment. We didn't speak first, which means we've taken the time to listen.

Not everybody in our rural communities is a believer—far from it. According to one analysis, only 54 percent of rural Americans identify as Christian.[9] But the bare statistics don't register that the deep connectedness of rural places means that rural people often understand themselves to belong to the community's founding religious groups whether, in Christian contexts, they attend Christmas and Easter or nothing at all. They might not believe, but they're Mennonite or Lutheran or Dutch Reformed. *Of course I am, with a last name like mine!* Alas.

In rural communities, we have to earn the right to speak. The question in rural communities is always—fairly or unfairly—*Are you one of us?*

I talked to a man who described how, after living in a small town for years, he had stood up at a community meeting to express his opinion. But before he could get a word out, the resident next to him said, "Sit down, you're not from here."

Cities are a big mix. People move to cities. There are circles upon circles of overlapping relations and unrelations. Walk the streets. Take the train. *Are you from here?* That's not an important question. Rural areas, on the other hand, understand themselves as known and knowable. Growth is a source of pride, but even so: *Are you one of us?*

What all of this means is that for Christians, the evangelistic habitus is a habitus of humility. We have the humility to speak gently, the humility to not have all the answers, the humility to take our time. It's a humility born of long walking with the God who takes his time and who doesn't give up on people.

But at some point, we have to speak.

I met a man once who became a Christian because at a low point in his life, as he stopped for gas while traveling, a complete stranger came up to him and gave him an evangelistic tract. He told me how he took that tract back to his hotel room and pored over it. And he gave his life to Christ. Tracts aren't supposed to work anymore. This is twenty-first-century North America, for Pete's sake! Our society is a postmodern something-or-other pastiche. Tracts? There's something almost gleefully ridiculous about the idea of an impersonal contact with a stranger foisting an impersonal tract on someone leading that person to question his bedrock life commitments and eternal destiny. But there it was: A method was better than no method.

We never know the full impact of our words, which is why we just have to use them. Release them like a flock of doves and see what happens.

We connect, and then we speak.

PRACTICING AUTHENTICITY

We do all of this connecting and speaking while practicing authenticity.

I strive to be authentic. It's one of my core values. I want to be real, be who I am, speak my truth. But authenticity is hard to measure. Whenever we do something new or perplexing, we're always going to feel a little inauthentic, and the same goes for evangelism in rural communities.

My wife and I once targeted a low-income apartment complex for personal evangelism. I suppose we were already off on an inauthentic foot by using the word *target*. But it was pretty simple: We went there and talked to people. Our little son played with the residents' kids. I took my bike and bike trailer once and gave the smaller children rides around the central patio.

One summer evening, the apartment manager came out. He knew we didn't live in those apartments. "Who are you?" he asked. "And what's your shtick?"

But that's just it: Cultivating an evangelistic habitus will mean precisely the opposite of having a shtick. It's watching for opportunities to connect with people for the sake of the gospel. In one way, connecting is its own end. We connect to connect. We start up a conversation with the new family on the sidelines. We introduce ourselves to the grocery store cashier. In rural communities, we have the luxury of taking our time because we're not anonymous to each other and there's a good chance we'll see that family or cashier again. We're just talking. There's no shtick.

In fact, I think we want to avoid having a shtick at all costs. Nothing turns people off more than the sense that we're not being honest about our motives. Nobody likes to feel like they're being used. You get a taste of this whenever a new individual or family visits a small rural congregation. We get so excited. We laugh a little too much. We corner them and crank our sparkling personalities up to ten. See you next week! (Fingers crossed.)

All of that can mean coming off as a little forced. It's not because we aren't authentically happy to have them in worship with us. We are. It's just anxiety that leads to a potential inauthenticity: that (let's be honest) our little country church needs every warm body we can get.

No doubt Jesus' words had such an immediate impact on people because of his authenticity. He was precisely who he was: the Son of God, the Beloved. With him the Father was well pleased (Mark 1:11). Jesus was comfortable in his own skin like no other human being who has ever lived. They would later say of him that he taught "as one having authority" (1:22). And so Jesus could do things like start up conversations with fishermen who were in their element, surrounded by their kin, and not come off as having some kind of itinerant evangelist shtick. When he said, "Follow me and I will make you fish for people" it made absolute, complete, and perfect sense (1:17). Deep called to deep (Psalm 42:7). What else could they do but follow?

This is where the wilderness intersects with the seashore. Jesus went deep with the Father before he called disciples. So it is with us. We'll need to cultivate a spacious place within ourselves, a place where we can live into becoming more truly ourselves, before we can ever hope to talk to people about the gospel. Prayer precedes evangelism.

This doesn't mean we have to be perfect at it. The notion that we should only do things that we have perfected comes from an anxious place in our cultural psyche. The apostle Paul has a different take on who should evangelize. He speaks of the role of evangelist as a gift, which means that there will always be those within the church who do evangelism unself-consciously (Ephesians 4:11). We do well to discern and affirm their gift. We should encourage our evangelists and commission them with the laying on of hands. Yet Paul also tells Timothy to "do the work of an evangelist," which I've always understood to mean that Timothy was not necessarily good at evangelizing—but he did the work anyway (2 Timothy 4:5).

That's me: the flawed evangelist if ever there was one, struggling to connect with people and speak the gospel truth and do it all with a non-shtickified authenticity. Who knows the impact we have on people? Who knows the soil our words will land on? The point is that we keep trying. As rural church leader Kent Anderson puts it, we "count the casts, not the fish."[10]

That summer evening at the apartment complex, after the manager asked me about my shtick, we ended up sitting at a concrete picnic table as moths clouded the lights, talking about life and death and faith and eternity. He even came to church once and brought some of his friends.

Who knows?

4

Listening and Telling Stories

Let anyone with ears to hear listen! —Mark 4:9

A prospective pastor couple once contacted the interim pastor of a nearby congregation we knew. They were interested in learning more about the open position at the church he was serving. They thought it might be a very good fit, not least because they loved the landscape of Washington State—all those pine forests blanketing the mountains with green. All those ancient blue glaciers creaking down the Cascades.

There was only one problem: the church was located in central Washington. Instead of lush pine forests, there were a million miles of sagebrush. Rather than mountains, there were hills and basalt gorges. Central Washington has a stark beauty all its own, especially in the spring when the sagebrush flowers and takes on a shy purple hue. But that, apparently, wasn't what they had in mind. They saw Washington as one thing, and they couldn't see the landscape for what it actually was.

There's little harm done when sagebrush hills are mistaken for pine forests. Everyone can have a good chuckle. But that little faux pas is a parable of something more subtle and sinister. It's all too easy to see rural communities and churches as one thing, to tell one story about them, thereby missing them for what they truly are and failing to accept them on their own terms.

Jesus showed a different way. He told great big stories full of meaning with lots of on- and off-ramps. The sower goes out to sow, but the soil might be stony or thistle-thick or patrolled by greedy-eyed birds. The bad luck trail runs in just the wrong place. The word may fall on the good and receptive soil, but there's no guarantee of growth—or understanding. Jesus' parables aren't nice little sermon illustrations meant to connect with an agrarian audience. They're so much more sly and disruptive than that. Jesus told parables so that "they may indeed look, but not perceive, and may indeed listen, but not understand" (Mark 4:12). His parables certainly aren't any one thing. "Let anyone with ears to hear listen!" (4:9).

Novelist Chimamanda Ngozi Adichie speaks of the "danger of a single story." To tell a single story is to "show a people as one thing, as only one thing, over and over again." The stories we tell fashion perceptions and shape identities, and thus when we tell a single story about a people, "that is what they become." As Adiche notes, "Power is the ability not just to tell the story of another person, but to make it the definitive story of that person."[1]

One of the gifts we give rural communities (or any community, for that matter) is an attentive presence that listens and tells stories. We attune our ears to the diversity and complexity of rural people and places. We refuse to tell a single story and instead allow ourselves to be schooled in telling frayed stories and beautiful stories and stories of struggle.

TELL FRAYED STORIES

If, as businessman Max De Pree argued, "the first responsibility of leadership is to define reality," then perhaps the first task of rural church leadership is to tell a different story.[2] Like Jesus, we need to tell big, frayed stories made up of many threads, stories in which there are all kinds of soil with all kinds of possibilities. Because the stories we tell will define our reality—or at least sketch its contours.

Philosopher Ludwig Wittgenstein posited that "the limits of my language mean the limits of my world."[3] We know things by naming them. We often can't think beyond the stories we tell about ourselves or the world. And so to know and serve rural places truly, we have to begin to tell complex stories about rural, frayed stories that don't necessarily resolve nicely.

We see this in the way Jesus tells stories. They're parables, a kind of story that avoids making any one simple point and invites the listener in. Are you the woman searching for the coin, or the sheep tangled in briars hoping the shepherd makes it in time? Are you the prodigal son or the son who stayed home or the father? Maybe it depends on what day of the week you hear the story. They're parables, not morality tales. They don't just make a point or illustrate a point or drive home a point. They catalyze the listener's moral and spiritual imagination.

Thus the parable of the sower in Mark 4:3–9. "Listen!" Jesus says. "A sower went out to sow." He broadcast seeds his field. When it falls on the path, the birds eat it. When it falls on the rocky ground, it withers for lack of root. When it falls among thorns, it is choked away before it can produce grain. But some of that precious seed falls on the good soil, and it yields "thirty and sixty and a hundredfold."

Jesus' parable is a story of abundance. The sower flings the seed regardless of the results. This sower takes an unstrategic approach, sowing abundantly. "The gospel is lavish—you might even say it's *wasteful*," writes Stephen Witmer.[4]

It seems to me that abundance is a good place to begin rural ministry. Were it not for the abundance of God, there would be no rural ministry. God's heart is found most fully at the margins, and rural is historically one (though not the only one) of those margins. There just aren't as many people, and thus rural cannot produce the cultural goods of society in the same way as the great cities. In ancient days, it was Rome's *honor, gloria,* and *dignitas.*[5] In our day, I suppose it's platform, prestige, and influence.

But this is to miss the point, for the abundance of the rural church is not produced by rural communities or congregations. It does not depend on how many interstate exits a place has. Rural abundance flows from the Father's abundant heart, and the lavish-gospel ministry of the rural church is a sign of Christ's abundant love for all people in all places, great and podunk small. It's no different for ministry in any place. All ministry—if it's sustained, if it's true, if, in the end, it's ministry at all—is ladled from God's abundant well. And God's love for all people and places is what girds us up and gives us the courage to go rural. It's why we take bivocational positions and put up with the smell of the feedlot and drive long distances for our groceries.

I met a Catholic priest who served a vast parish in rural Montana. He celebrated Mass in one congregation, hurriedly shook hands at the back of the sanctuary, then hit the road to drive hours to his second congregation. Who would sign up for something like that if not for some palpable sense of God's abundant love? It's the Sower dipping his hand into the bag and drawing out fistfuls of seed and seed and seed. More than enough seed for every soil. The word of God to all peoples. The Great Sower doesn't give up even if the soil isn't all perfect. Every inch of it is worthy of the seed.

Once, during a Bible study in college, I happened to glance over at my friend's Bible. He was the kind of guy who scribbles notes in the margins, and next to the parable of the sower, he had written, "What kind of soil am I?"

It's a fair enough question. What eager disciple, on hearing this parable, doesn't long to be the good soil, the rich humus free of birds and rocks and thorns that receives the seed and produces stalks that hang heavy with grain?

There's just one thing: soil doesn't get to decide what it is. It certainly doesn't get to cultivate itself. If you've got rocky soil, you've got rocky soil. You don't throw wheat at it. You become a rancher. If you've got birds, you go hunting. If you've got thorns—well, I recommend goats. But the soil is what it is.

Like my college friend, I've mainly read this parable as a story of personal self-improvement. But there's something very American and middle-class about such a reading, and I'm skeptical that's how Jesus intended it. The older I get, the more the parable of the sower seems like a story of acceptance. We don't get to control how or why or where the seed of the word falls. We don't pick our results. To sow or not to sow, that is the question—which, of course, is really no question at all.

Leaders of small rural congregations face a challenge in this. We're called to stand in a minor paradox. On the one hand, we serve rural congregations by meeting them where they're at. We accept them, which means seeing a place for what they are, in all their complicated glory. "To love your neighbor is to see your neighbor," writes theologian Frederick Buechner. We come with curiosity and ask our congregation and our community the simple and profound and probing question: "How did *you* happen?"[6] Because in every way, things could be different: a different congregation with a different cast of characters in a different sort of town. But the river or the train or the end of the valley, and it was *you*.

In taking a posture of acceptance, we can risk giving up on our mandate to call congregations to something more. That's the flip side. We're supposed to dream big, too. But I wonder whether this little conundrum isn't in fact a failure to tell frayed stories. Yes, we do our best work. Yes, we bring our very best imaginations and burning heart passion for God and God's people. But we're just humble under-sowers who don't get to decide where the seed lands or how it grows. We can't see the full implications of what we're doing or how we're doing it. We just sow.

In *The Horse and His Boy* by C. S. Lewis, there's a moment when Aslan, the Christ figure, is asked the perennial *Why?* There are two horses, and one is wounded and the other is not. Why did what happened, happen? But no, it is not for one horse to know why the other horse suffered. The great lion Aslan responds: "I tell no one any story but his own."[7]

There's a truth in that. We never know the fullness of the story that God is telling in the life of another. We nearly always underestimate it, reducing it to a thread of what we can see. What's more, to know our own story is a great gift that few of us manage to receive. It's become clear(er) to me over the years that the reasons I think God called me to the places I've served and the reasons I've actually been in those places haven't always run parallel. When I'm a black-and-white portrait on the fellowship hall wall, what will they remember me for? The weightiest things I've been involved with also happen to be least likely to garner recognition.

Jesus told a story with four kinds of soil, each with their own ending and only one thing in common: they encountered the sower. It's not a children's story, not Goldilocks finding her just-right soil. It's the seed scattering in all different places, embedding in all sorts of hearts, and we never know any story except maybe, by God's grace, our own. Which means, I think, that we need to begin to challenge the ways that rural stories have been told. We need to complicate the rural story and move away from simplicities that cram rural communities and congregations into our expectations. We unravel the single story by telling a frayed story of rural.

All too often, the single story told about rural—a story more likely than not told by the city—is a story that is something less than abundant. More likely than not, it's a story of decline.

True, some rural communities are on the decline. Especially since J. D. Vance's breakout book *Hillbilly Elegy*, which describes the rough-and-tumble economic hardship in the hollers of Appalachia where the author grew up, there's been a tendency in certain circles to paint everything west of Pittsburgh and east of Sacramento with a monochrome brush. Grandma's rural town is falling apart fast, and the smartest kids are getting out even faster. It's the Narrative of Rural Decline, a tale rooted in a reading of rural North America that posits urban life as the apex of civilization and urban cultures and politics as having a sort of evolutionary momentum and finality. It's *Hillbilly Elegy* on steroids, a narrative that has no space for thriving small towns and communities. Pick your state and you can find it: Exhibit A (and B and C) of rural decline—the crumbling downtown, the trickling away population, the trees punching out the windows of the abandoned schoolhouse. I've seen these communities, witnessed these trends.

But there are also abundant cases of what sociologist Benjamin Winchester playfully calls "brain gain." In a nifty reversal of the standard narrative, it turns out that in many rural communities, the percentage of residents between age thirty and forty-nine has increased. The population seems to dip among twenty-somethings as young people head to college and graduate school, but then many of these folks marry and return to rural—or others relocate to rural—to raise their families and be part of their home community. These returners and relocators bring with them professional degrees, salaries, and leadership potential.[8]

This trend accelerated during the COVID-19 pandemic, with people moving out of high-density cities for suburbs, small towns, and rural communities.[9] I talked to a pastor whose small town in Vermont experienced a sudden spike in people relocating from New York City, with waiting lists for apartments running twenty deep.[10]

When I first discovered that many rural communities were growing, I could hardly accept it. I had been indoctrinated into the notion that rural was universally on the decline. Signs of that decline seemed obvious enough in my community: for a several-year period in the 2010s, our downtown restaurants and coffee shop had closed, talk around town was that we might need to consolidate the school with a larger nearby community, and the housing market seemed frozen.

Yet that wasn't the only story. Unemployment was (and is) nil. One newspaper article documented that local industries generate some 1,500 jobs—this in a community whose population had only just bumped 1,800 people at the time (it is now closer to 2,000).[11] Which is to say: there are more jobs than working adults. New kids keep appearing in my sons' classes, a trend which only accelerated during the pandemic as families sought in-person schooling options. When I dressed up as Moses—complete with cardboard Ten Commandments—and handed out candy at our annual trick-or-treat street event, to my astonishment, I didn't know two-thirds of the children. Not long ago, a new Mexican restaurant moved in, and a hip coffee and pizza place opened up at the four corners downtown. Good luck finding a house to buy or apartment to rent in my community—or any rural town for a fifty-mile radius.

Interestingly, the decline that is supposed to have taken place across rural communities where my Mennonite tradition has a historic footprint hasn't played out the way denominational leaders have imagined. Many communities in the Mennonite heartlands have actually grown, though the traditional congregations located in these communities have for the most part shrunk.

I get pushback whenever I talk about these countervailing trends. Once, in a workshop on rural mission and evangelism, an older gentleman admitted that new people had moved to his community. "But," he said, "they're rough people." There are often more new people—rough or otherwise—in our communities than we realize. The census numbers are hard to argue with. I name this not to make us feel guilty about our congregation's lack of growth, but to prod us to ask what story we're telling about our community and whether it jibes with reality.

In the same way, we can fall into telling a single story of the rural church. It goes something like this: rural congregations are has-beens, dilapidated little ministry outposts that got stuck on bell choirs and have long needed a bass-beat blood transfusion. Sometimes, the dilapidated and stuck part is true enough—though I question whether this is a rural phenomenon. All churches tend to get frozen at a certain phase in their life cycle.

However, there are scads of stories to the contrary. Just down the road from us, a colleague has been leading his traditional congregation in a remarkable rejuvenation. He hasn't implemented any high-octane plan; he has simply preached solid sermons and cultivated a non-anxious presence. And the congregation has a rocking multigenerational bell choir.

TELL BEAUTIFUL STORIES

A lot of rural towns have museums. Ours does. It's a meandering, well-cared for stroll through the history of our community. They've got the old newspaper printing press with its lead type, signs from the old dairy, chairs from the old barber shop. There are tractors and farm implements and a working blacksmith shop.

What I love about these small-town museums is how you'll see signs for them on the interstate exits. It takes a superb kind of self-confidence to envision folks pulling off the highway to get a taste of our history. I once heard a motivational speaker at a local event who had even grander aspirations for rural museums. He was a Big Ideas kind of guy who talked about the role of technology in our lives. The man trotted out some nifty gadgets, including a two-wheeled, long-stemmed thing that you could mount a tablet on. He imagined a day when this device would mosey its gyroscope-balanced way through the nursing home halls so that the grandkids could chat with Grandma. And—imagine it!—what if we used it to give automated tours of the historical museum? We could program it to run at night. Chinese school children on the dayside of the world would tune in to see our museum. I was stunned in the very best way by the audacity of the idea, his conviction that the world wants to hear our story.

We want to be heard. We want our story to be known, and not just in the quirky way that museums tell it. I think we long for the Godward bits of our story to be listened to and affirmed and drawn out.

One of the things I admire about charismatic Christians is how they tell their stories as miracle stories. My story is more modest. I grew up in the faith and committed the usual hackneyed and unoriginal sins (the way all sin is in fact hackneyed and unoriginal) and experienced grace in its saturating, fresh, percolating, subversive, slow ways. Charismatics whom I have met speak of light and darkness, of that moment when grace blitzed their life and they knew themselves to be stepping into something new. They speak of dreams and visions and healings. Their lives are miracle stories, accented by the divine.

I think we all want something like this. We all want to tell about the miracles. What's more, we want the miracle that is our life to be told. This is us in all our amazing us-ness, and everybody should pull off the interstate to hear our story. People on the other side of the world should take a gyroscope-balanced tour of our lives.

And here we are, pastors and leaders with front-row seats on the same side of the world to the story of a place. Are we listening? Are we noticing the manifold ways that God walks quietly through our lives, through the life of our rural church and community? Or do we enter in with brains like moles, rooting our way through things, blindly burrowing for problems and never noticing the varieties of soil?

Because the soil is not incidental to Jesus' parable. Soil necessarily implies place. It's the placedness of our lives, the way that place shapes us. Human beings are always beings in place. This is especially true of rural people, who hold "a remarkable and unflinching sense of place."[12] The gospel touches upon a place in all our uniqueness and challenge and struggle. That's the kind of story we have to tell. We have to tell those distinctively rural stories that open up the reductionist origami to which rural has been subjected by our urbanized society. We need to tell the beautiful stories of our rural communities and congregations: the way it seems like every business lets you buy things on credit, the food market delivering groceries to shut-in elders, the hot dish left on the porch during a pandemic quarantine, the hay farmer rushing stacks of enormous round bales to ranchers after devastating wildfires.

We tell the beautiful stories of rural because they're the true stories. They're stories that point to something beyond themselves. Nature too: "The whole earth is full of his glory" (Isaiah 6:3). Those speckled hens aren't just chickens. That cloud like an alligator half-submerged in the sky is no mere stratocumulus. Your town, your congregation. Yourself. They're more than they seem: specks of grace, signs of God's *something more*. "Beauty and grace are performed whether or not we will or sense them," erstwhile prophet Annie Dillard writes. "The least we can do is try to be there."[13] Which means that telling true and beautiful stories entails a kind of presence. We're being there. We're showing up to place and people with christoform eyes able to see and ears that can hear that-of-God in our congregation and community and life, able to tease out how God's story twines through ours. To tell the beautiful story of a place is to begin to see it truly and to love what God has called good.

TELL STORIES OF STRUGGLE

And yet.

To speak truly of rural people and places is also to tell stories of struggle. Jesus belongs to the Brutally Honest School of

Parabolizing. Three out of four types of soil lead to creatively envisioned disaster. The word faces long odds.

Years ago, I slipped into a standing-room-only university lecture hall to hear a famous biologist. He was talking about ecosystems and adaptation, and (I don't know why I remember this line) he said that you can be the most exquisitely adapted fish in your ecosystem, but if your puddle dries up, you end up just as dead. That strikes me as a parable of the church in rural communities. There are places that are struggling, where the schools were consolidated half a generation ago and the kids and sports and financial focus shifted elsewhere. The shuttered school building leans in slow-motion toward the ground behind weeds and barbed wire. Some of the congregations were exquisitely adapted to life in the 1950s; some were geared toward reaching out to a large multiethnic population drawn by work in the local chicken-processing plant. But the puddle dried up. The plant closed and the people left and the pastor became a postman. We have to tell those stories too.

Of course, such storytelling involves risk. If we're not careful, we can end up joining the ranks of voyeurs of rural decline (not to be outdone by the lock-the-doors-and-just-keep-driving voyeurs of urban decline). I once pulled off the road in a tiny blip of a town in western Kansas. I found myself standing in a post-apocalyptic pulp scene. An icy fog blanketed everything. Wildfires smoldered on the invisible horizon, and ash drifted onto my arm hairs. I crunched across the gravel and snapped pictures of the demolished school, gone but for an impressive concrete arch entryway. The signs on another building labeled it a church youth center. Its roof had caved in long ago, and what remained sagged dangerously. I wanted to see this place, but I felt self-conscious, a little embarrassed to be playing the journalist with my camera in hand. What story would I be telling with my pictures? I slipped back into my car and disappeared into the mist.

When we tell stories of struggle, it can be easy to fixate on struggle, to succumb to the toxicity of pity, to tell the story with a slant for the bottom. A suburban congregation once sent their youth group on a mission trip to the town I served. I liked it. But I didn't. What kind of story were they telling about our community, just by showing up? (But then again, we took our youth to Seattle for their mission trip, so maybe fair's fair).

There are ways to tell the story of that sagging Kansas church building without resorting to melodrama. We step right into the middle of the brokenness and tell it straight up. There is struggle. Churches struggle. Communities come apart at the seams.

Why tell these stories? It's not to write off rural as backwards and has-been places, places that failed to adapt and thus somehow deserve what they got. We tell struggle stories for the same reason we speak to beauty: because God is there. Struggle is part of the story of God-with-us too. Things fall apart. . . . And yet.

This is the testimony of the Scriptures. Read anywhere in 1 Samuel through Nehemiah—just pick a passage at random. There's a good chance you'll flip to a story of things falling apart: Eli's wicked sons run Shiloh and the Philistines capture the ark. Saul grows impatient. David spots Bathsheba. O Absalom! The kingdom splits under Rehoboam. And on and so on. Josiah's senseless death. Assyria and Sennacherib. It's not the fall that kills your kingdom but the sudden stop at Babylon.

And yet: David and Elijah and Elisha and Ahijah and people like Jeremiah who, when the walls of the city lean in slow motion and the kingdom tatters, still spot God, still speak of him. "There is something like a burning fire shut up in my bones," says Jeremiah; "I am weary with holding it in, and I cannot" (Jeremiah 20:9). Birds, boulders, briars—still they sow.

I remember reading the story of a famous church planter and man of God. He describes hunkering down in the basement of his seminary library and researching the fastest-growing part of the country. Then he set off to skillfully plant a church there. It sprung up and yielded thirty and sixty and a hundredfold. I was duly inspired.

But for the church to truly be the church, we're going to do in an internet-fast way what that pastor did in analog—but for the smallest, farthest, fastest-shrinking places. We're going to go where the horizon is burning and the walls are sagging, where ravenous birds murmurate and gravel roads snake and thistles smother the ruins of the school. The church will always go rural, because that's where Christ himself goes. The story of the rural church is a story of God in the struggle.

We see the struggle and name the struggle and enter into the heart of the struggle. We recognize resilience and find those little plots where the seed courageously springs up, in spite of it all. In this way, to tell a story of struggle is to see our story resolve into beauty.

I know a pastor who came to serve a little country church. She had previously helped a congregation close its doors. "Have they called you to close this church?" I asked as she was settling in. No. She recognized the enormous headwinds the congregation was facing, and she went there anyway. It felt like a gracious act of sowing, of pouring herself out on behalf of a congregation that despite her best efforts and best strategies and best preaching might remain a small rural congregation—or might even close its doors.

Thus it is. The rural church is always teetering between a rock and a demographic hard place.

And yet.

Christ went there first.

5

Walking on Water. Or Not.

He intended to pass them by. —Mark 6:48

I've failed a lot. I don't mean so much moral failure, though I confess daily to almighty God and to you my brothers and sisters that I have greatly sinned, in my thoughts and in my words, in what I have done and in what I have failed to do. I have plenty of material. But the failures (that I'm willing to tell you about) have mostly been failures to know what to do and how to do it. My best failures have come when I've taken risks and failed. Those have been the moments when I've felt that, however far the drop, at least I took a swing on the trapeze. Though, to be honest, there have been other times when I've looked out the window of my comfort zone, hunkered down, pulled up the blankets, and said *Not today*. Sometimes I've failed to take the big and worthy risk.

What I've discovered along the way is this: dynamic rural ministry is risk-taking and open to failure. What's more, we get better at risk-taking and failure with practice, and at some point they become part of who we are. I've failed a lot, and you can too!

Two conversations early in my ministry shaped my sense of failure. The first was a sit-down with a key congregational leader. I was learning to know everyone, just starting to get the slimmest inkling of the lay of the land, when in the middle of our conversation he told me in not so many words: "We're in a crisis!" That got my heart beating. I hadn't detected that our congregation was in crisis mode. Sure, we were small. But we had a slew of home-grown kids, committed young leaders, a couple of wise elders lending stability and wisdom, and the pastor was getting paid. It didn't seem like a crisis to me. However, I learned that before I arrived, the congregation had lost some people because of (as far as I could rough in the narrative) a presidential election, discontent over conference positions around human sexuality, and the residue of changing to a new hymnal. So we were in crisis. Cortisol was in the air, and my empathetic heart bounded down the rabbit hole to try to fix everything for everybody.

I began trying one thing after another. I tinkered. I called multiple congregational visioning meetings and out of them plotted bold directions forward involving lots of volunteers, lots of money, and lots of risky changes. I envisioned a community center engaging the youth and a community organizer who would work with families around immigration issues. Some good directions came out of it, but mostly, things got really wobbly, really fast.

Which led to my second conversation. One of the church's stable and wise elders came to me and told me: "I think people would be more willing to follow you in the things you're proposing if they could see some results." But of course, that was the problem. I didn't know what would get results. I was trying everything, throwing spaghetti at the walls to see what would stick. I didn't know what to do or how to do it. I was failing often and fast, and when my (quirkily short) first term was up at year two, I very nearly threw in the towel.

CHURCH X

You would think my try-everything approach would have at least put me in good company—if not on the right track. After all, it was around the same time when the biggest companies and most innovative leaders were recommending a "fail often, fail well" approach.[1] The big idea was that innovation can happen only when organizations create a culture where it's okay to fail, where failure is celebrated. Astro Teller, head of X, formerly Google X, the technology giant's "moonshot" division that seeks to solve global problems with out-of-the-box technological solutions, describes how his organization encourages its employees to "fail fast." They applaud inventors and engineers who try big things and fail. They award bonuses and promote workers who fail. Teller speaks of giving hugs and high-fives to employees who fail. All of this based on a philosophy that sees failure as the coefficient of the creative destruction of risk-taking.[2]

But let me tell you: I wasn't getting no hugs and high-fives. My congregation was quickly becoming tetchy and exhausted. Nothing seemed to produce results. My Church X fail-fast strategy wasn't moving us where we needed to go, and honestly, I wasn't even sure where I wanted to get us.

What's more, I was doubting my call and engaging in a whole lot of rotten self-examination. I began to think that maybe I didn't have what it took for success in ministry. I longed for something that would jazz up my leadership and rev our worship attendance. Somebody told me I just needed to get filled with the Holy Spirit as manifested by speaking in tongues. Someone else suggested I borrow a page from that

TV pastor with the feel-good message and the Texas-size congregation. One pastor blithely told me that I just needed to preach the Bible. I couldn't recall preaching anything but.

It was, however, the Bible that set me straight. I had become entangled in a kind of leadership scrupulosity. I should have known better. At some level, I did know better, because I knew the stories. I had read the Scriptures. I treasured them in my heart that I might not sin against God, as Psalm 119:11 instructs. And the God I saw in those Scriptures—when I paused from visioning long enough to remember and get recentered—was a God of the fail, the Mighty One who promises to take our most unmighty and unpromising materials and fashion something good.

Perhaps nowhere is this more clear than in the gospel account of the disciples struggling in the storm and Jesus walking on the water. In Mark 6, Jesus tells the disciples to get into the boat and cross the sea. Actually, the Greek word is more to the point: Jesus "forced" them to do it (Mark 6:45). He compelled them. It's the same word for the master telling his servant to "compel" the least and the lost to come to his grand banquet (Luke 14:23). It's what Paul did in his Bad Saul days when he "tried to *force* them to blaspheme" (Acts 26:11). In the Apocrypha, it's the word underwriting Antiochus's reign of terror. His men seized Jews and attempted "to *compel* them to eat pork and food sacrificed to idols" (4 Maccabees 5:2; see also 2 Maccabees 7:1). With this word, the gospel is subtly telling us that Jesus set the disciples up for an experience of failure. He aimed their boat at the jaws of defeat, put his foot against the stern, and shoved them off. The Lord be with you and best of luck. Then he "went up on the mountain to pray" (Mark 6:46).

As evening descends, an "adverse wind" picks up. The disciples are "straining against the oars" (6:48). Just earlier that day, Jesus had called the disciples to retreat so that they could "rest a while" (6:31). Now he prays alone through the night while they struggle. Matthew 14:24 tells us that they were "battered by the waves." I imagine the disciples: wet, cold, exhausted, and far from land. I imagine their boat fast taking on water, their oar strokes less effective with every heave. Their faith is a tattered little wind-whipped thing. Hope fell overboard an hour ago. Until Jesus comes to them in a miracle of epic proportions, striding across the sea. They are saved! Except. This: "He intended to pass them by" (Mark 6:48).

Oh yes he did.

That statement is Mark's little stick of theodicean dynamite, and I'm tempted to psychologize it away: the disciples *thought* he was passing them by. Or I want to storybook it: by passing them by, Jesus was setting the disciples up to look to him, to set their eyes on him, to trust in him. But both explanations fall short of the real strangeness of the passage.

Scholar Joel Marcus notes that at the time of the Gospels, the word for *pass by* had "become almost a technical term for a divine epiphany" in the Greek Old Testament.[3] The archetypal story of God passing by Moses while the prophet hides in the cleft of the rock sets the terms for a God who reveals himself to humanity and yet never fully discloses himself (Exodus 33:17–34:8). The God who passes Moses by passes Elijah by as well (1 Kings 19:11–13). And now Jesus, who will be flanked by Moses and Elijah at the Transfiguration, comes to the disciples across the water, intending to pass them by. "Who then is this, that even the wind and the sea obey him?" (Mark 4:41).

Matthew famously adds that Peter calls out to the Lord, angling for an invitation to walk on the water with him. But "when he noticed the strong wind, he became frightened, and beginning to sink, he cried out, 'Lord, save me!'" (Matthew 14:30). It's a fail story within a fail story. The disciples fail to navigate the storm and fail to make it across the Sea of Galilee and fail to even recognize Jesus. Peter fails to stand on his own two soaked feet. And Jesus intended to pass them by.

All of this to say that something more is going on when Jesus calls us out onto the wet and wavy places to follow him—places ripe for failure. Writes Deborah Gorton: "We've allowed failure to become this unspeakable disaster that must be avoided at all costs, because the outcome is more than we can handle or even survive."[4] We're acculturated to avoid failure at all costs. But sometimes, it's precisely into failure and unspeakable disaster that Jesus launches us, and this is why we need to reimagine failure and reconceive how we can move forward in hope through it.

PACING FOR RURAL MINISTRY

When I asked small-town Lutheran pastor Tim Koch about advice for rural pastors and leaders, his first recommendation was this: "Do nothing quickly."[5] It's good advice. And it runs smack in the face of the "fail fast" corporate vogue.

Pacing matters in rural ministry in large part because rural congregations and communities have seen it all before: the hotshot young pastor with the latest ideas swooping in to make Big Changes and then moving on when things don't pan out. Local leaders fill in the gaps when the pastor leaves, and each time it happens they become stronger and more essential and coyote-warier of change. They're *conservative* in the truest sense of the word: desiring to conserve their congregation's treasures and heritage.

What's more, congregations and communities that have experienced decline come to frame life differently. Their expectations of what's possible shift, and it becomes challenging to get excited about new ideas. So many visions have fizzled, so many plans crumbled. It's a kind of collective trauma, and leadership in these rural communities will always require an empathetic angle. Rural church leadership is always healing work.

One way for pastors to undertake this healing work is by sticking around long enough to prove that they're safe, that they have the congregation's best interests at heart, that they're not going to pick up and head out at the first sign of trouble. Longevity foments trust. The longer we stay put, the clearer it becomes that pastors aren't answer men and women who know the secret sauce for success if only this creaky old congregation would demonstrate a little get-up-and-go. We don't know what's going to happen. It's all too tempting and easy to pull out when things don't go as planned. Leaving gives pastors a comfortable cover story: we're good leaders, the fault is with the congregation. God called us elsewhere when they wouldn't follow our lead.

But to be open to failure is to be with the people in whatever happens. It's also to celebrate every little success. We encourage. We tell stories of hope. In this way, rural pastors and leaders create spaces where risk-taking and the possibility of failure can be safely processed. It's the methodically slow work of helping congregations imagine a different future. As even Astro Teller of X says: "You cannot yell at people and force them to fail fast."[6]

Because in moments of crisis, the temptation for pastors is to show "strong leadership," to stand out front, leading lantern-jawed into the gale. We'll be tempted to make chipper claims like "This is actually an opportunity!" Or "I think we can grow through this if we just [fill in the blank on the vision ideogram]." And there's pressure on leaders to be that vision-person. Isn't that what they pay us for? "Where there is no vision, the people perish," don't you know? (Proverbs 29:18 KJV). But really, we're just a bunch of guys on a spinning boat in a storm who can't tell the difference between the Lord of the Universe and a spook. Even ever-ready Peter can't handle the wind and the waves.

FAILURE AND VULNERABILITY

Failure is not an altogether practical matter that can be circumscribed by vision and metrics. There's an irreducible mystery to failure. The reality is that when we talk about ministry, we hardly know what failure is.

Though I suppose in one way, we do know. Failure is as failure does. There's moral failure. There's lack of drive, lack of initiative, half-baked vision, and half-hearted work. Pastor J. R. Briggs, founder of the Epic Fail Conference, writes about four distinct types of failure: the mighty fall, tragic event, slow leak, or burned-out statistic.[7] Congregations can fail to reach out in their communities, fail to welcome newcomers, fail to cling to Christ and his word. But none of those garden varieties of failure is particularly interesting. They're easily identifiable. Every failing leader knows to avoid them. I suppose every failing church knows what it's supposed to be about too. The problem comes when we begin to see success as a product of our own drive and skill and effort and moxie—and failure as our lack thereof.

But Jesus sends us places where drive, skill, effort, and moxie will falter, will sink, will—well—fail. Ministry is the willingness to obey Jesus' word, get in the boat, and start paddling even though we can see with our own two eyes that a storm is brewing on the horizon.

Partly this is because in ministry, we never really know what Jesus is doing through us and our congregation. We won't always know why he sent us out in that boat. Jesus has his own plans and goals and secret ways to achieve them. "Who has known the mind of the Lord? Or who has been his counselor?" says Romans 11:34 (NIV). We just don't have the vantage to fit the events that happen in and around us into God's convoluted providence, much less to label something a failure. "Do not pronounce judgment before the time, before the Lord comes, who will bring to light the things now hidden in darkness and will disclose the purposes of the heart," writes the apostle Paul. "Then each one will receive commendation from God" (1 Corinthians 4:5). What looks like failure may produce fruits in ways we hadn't imagined or anticipated.

Andrew Bermudez is a Baptist pastor in small-town Dexter, Maine. Pastor Bermudez is by any measure carrying out a very successful ministry. He's making a tremendous impact on his community, not least by connecting deeply in the life of Dexter as a substitute teacher and coach and by serving on the town council. He's spearheading a downtown outreach center that will serve as a clearinghouse to connect folks in need to local resources and financial assistance.[8]

But before he came to Dexter, Pastor Bermudez experienced a rough spot in his ministry—a time that left him and his family stressed out, financially imperiled, and exhausted. He described how the stress caused him to develop sores all over his skin. Their newborn second child required near constant medical attention. A good night's sleep was a distant memory. By God's grace, that difficult chapter closed, and the calling to Dexter opened.

At the farewell party, the congregation's youth didn't mention anything that he had taught them. However, one thing did stand out to them about their pastor's time at the church: how he carried himself through the struggle and hardship. They saw him live out his faith. Pastor Bermudez told me that instead of asking "Why is this happening to me?," he has learned to ask "What am I supposed to be teaching here? What am I supposed to be learning here?" God calls us to follow courageously, to obey in faith. We just don't have the wherewithal to determine that we have failed.

Nowhere is this more true than in the rural church, where we are called upon to move out and away from the usual scaffolding of success. We're called to love dying things and to come to be at home with uncertainty. We'll throw our best everything into the church and sometimes watch as our congregation slides from seventy-five to sixty to (well, we stopped counting). *Now what, Lord?*

In a deep sense, all ministry is a kind of failure because ministry is to die to self and live to Christ (Philippians 1:21). All discipleship is this death. We die, and our lives are "hidden with Christ in God" (Colossians 3:3). Ministry's prerequisite is taking up our cross as Jesus instructs us in Mark 8:34 and following him, which is a kind of intentional failure. We're choosing to die to the world's definitions of success and failure when we take up our crosses. In that way, ministry is a kind of un-mastery, a slow dying to our sense of power and control. We die to having our expectations met by the church and the community. I don't think it's possible to minister from a place of authenticity without first tasting this death. And this death takes repetition and practice. "I die every day!" writes Paul in 1 Corinthians 15:31. Without this death, we'll always be covering for ourselves, always puffing out our chests, always making excuses or blaming the church. To die this death will lead to disillusionment, but only because we've been so illusioned by the world. Our sense of self dies, but we realize that it was always cardboard and two-dimensional anyway.

I suspect that the very concept of failure is a modern development clinking along on the mechanical wheels of our project-driven mindset. Project-driven works for some things, but rural ministry is likely not one of them. Doing rural ministry faithfully and well requires a certain fluidity. It's a willingness to move with the rhythms of community and congregation. This is hard to get right. I certainly haven't mastered it. I think this fluidity is about learning to gauge the potential for change in a system. It's about developing a pastoral intuition for where people are at and being willing to lead them from that point. When we begin to learn the ropes of this supple approach to ministry, then the appropriate drive to excellence, to challenge and innovate, flows from a place of humility and love for the people rather than from the insecurities of our ambition.

Failure strikes a tender place for pastors. Failure threatens the heart of our identity because it casts a shadow on our sense of being chosen by God. If God is with us, who can be against us (Romans 8:31)? Right? You are my son, my daughter, with you I am well pleased (Mark 1:11). We're more than conquerors (Romans 8:37). We confess the guaranteed victory of the almighty God, yet we know the clear and present reality of things falling apart in our lives and ministries. Too many pastors get pinched in the dissonance.

No doubt this is why whenever I talk to rural pastors, so many of them are contemplating quitting. They just want to get through the next crisis, and then they'll go out and get a regular job. They want something they don't have to justify to naysayers, something where they can get their hands dirty, leave the work at work, and go home.

Our misguided attitudes around failure wound churches as well. Because while Christ will never forsake his bride, and the church universal will reign victoriously with God forever, no such guarantee translates into the life of the local congregation. This is a feature, not a bug. The church is dependent on God. It is God's Spirit that fills and enlivens the church, God's word that the church speaks, God's work that the church undertakes with God's energy (1 Corinthians 3:16; 1 Peter 4:11). The church signs with its very life what it looks like to be dependent on God in all things. This dependence leaves open the possibility that God can take back his breath, and a congregation returns to the dust (Psalm 104:29–30). Failure isn't the right word here, because churches can be faithful to the end and still disappear. But congregations do die.

In my experience, the only way through all this failure is vulnerability. Vulnerability is the key skill: for dealing with the insecurity, for piercing the disillusionment, for learning to become ourselves. Whenever I've had the opportunity to speak to pastors and rural leaders, I start off saying something to the effect of *I really don't know what I'm doing.* I say this because my limitations are glaringly obvious to me. I know what I hope to achieve as a pastor—and all the ways I haven't managed to achieve it. And so it's either put up a facade, pretend to be the have-it-together pastor, or be transparent, be open, be vulnerable. I keep choosing vulnerability, and nobody's walked out yet. (Maybe they think I'm just being modest.)

Vulnerability is something we grow into, a way of life that we cultivate through the renunciative practices that Jesus taught in the Sermon on the Mount: giving, prayer, and fasting (Matthew 6:1–21). It's very nearly a spiritual discipline unto itself. In rural ministry, vulnerability looks like being honest about the struggles we and our congregations face. Vulnerability means learning to talk (in appropriate contexts) about those struggles—the places we feel stuck, the myriad ways we don't know what we're doing. Vulnerability involves a faith factor. We're embracing Paul's vulnerable words in 2 Corinthians 12:9: "My grace is sufficient for you, for power is made perfect in weakness."

Ultimately, vulnerability also sounds a hopeful note, because when we practice authentic vulnerability, we take the focus off of ourselves and our capabilities and shift it back to the God who can accomplish "abundantly far more than all we can ask or imagine" with the humble materials of our lives (Ephesians 3:20). Our wounds belong to God. Our weaknesses belong to God. Even our deaths—as individuals and congregations—can build the kingdom in God's turnabout providence. As J. R. Briggs puts it: "Ministry is fertile ground for failure, and failure is fertile ground for ministry."[9]

Brenda Henson is the pastor of an Assemblies of God congregation in tiny Greenville, Missouri. When we spoke, Pastor Henson described how she and her husband planted a new congregation in Greenville, a community near where she grew up. An Assemblies church had recently been shuttered in Greenville, though a few of the elder saints from the previous congregation were still around. *Why did this happen?* they asked. *Why didn't God revive our church?* Indeed, why plant a church where one had so recently died? Yet Henson and her small congregation persisted, and the new ministry grew to include a thrift store, a coffee shop (which later morphed into a game room), a thriving youth program, and a Narcotics

Anonymous group meeting in their community center.[10] When the previous congregation became vulnerable to closure and Pastor Henson became vulnerable to taking a risk on a new work, a fresh shoot grew from a dead trunk. Why? Only God knows.

SUCCESS AND PUSH-THROUGH

We struggle to understand failure, but we don't entirely know what success is either. We think we know because we've seen the glossy magazines. We've driven by the churches. Success looks like *that*, or at least a rural version of *that*. And who's to say? Those churches do represent a kind of success. If it's growing and vital and beautiful, then celebrate it.

But there's always the risk of doing all sorts of grand things but failing at the one thing needful. Take your pick of fallen Big Pastors, the rammers and jammers whom church and society love to lionize (before they fell, anyway). Too often, they reveal how in the most important and smallest ways, our priorities are formed by how we choose to occupy our days and weeks and years. Are we teaching people to pray? Are we growing in personal holiness? Are we pastoring our congregation—and maybe even our community—by taking that all-important first step of showing up and being present?

Over the years, I've reached out to rural and small church pastors, searching for the secret sauce to church thriving. I'm struck by how often they say the same thing: "There is no secret sauce." The secret is that there is no secret. Get involved in the community. Talk to people. Pray for them.

Oh, and one more thing: struggle.

Somewhere along the line, nearly every pastor of a currently thriving rural congregation experienced hardship or conflict or failure. When I jump on a Zoom call with these pastors to learn how they led their churches to thrive, we meander into this little jag in the conversation in which they relate the hard time that came before the good.

You see, so much of success and failure is wrapped up in the timeline. We think in terms of months and years, votes and projects and contracts, when we should be thinking in terms of lifetimes. Even addressing systemic injustice, like rural food deserts that develop when a community's last grocery store closes its doors, requires long-arc staying power and relationships built on years of trust. For instance, some rural towns have pioneered self-serve grocery store models to address community needs. That's not an overnight fix; it requires deep listening and long-term solidarity and neighborliness.[11] Oftentimes, our horizon is too short, and thus we believe that the latest roadblock is failure and the latest win success. But kick the goalpost back a decade, maybe even a century, and *then* we'll start to get a feel for success and failure—and our part in either.

I think of Adoniram Judson, the American Baptist missionary who in the 1830s began work among the Karen people of Burma (present-day Myanmar). For years, Judson didn't have a single convert to show for his struggle and hard living in Burma. Several of his infant children died. His wife died. He remarried, and his second wife died. He was imprisoned under horrific conditions during the Anglo-Burmese War. But years later, Christian faith would catch fire among the Karen people. Judson's translation of the Bible into Burmese would become the standard. Today, Myanmar boasts one of the largest Baptist populations in the world.[12]

Did Judson consider himself a failure in those early years? Did he ever think, "I'm pretty sure God doesn't want me here, which is why these things are happening to me"? Did he ever say, "I don't have the skills needed to see this project through"?

What would you do? Would you stay if you struggled with the language? If you had no converts? Would you stay if your child died? If your spouse died? If your second spouse died? If you were imprisoned and hung upside down in chains? I think I would have been on the next boat to New York.

True, we're not all going to be Judsons whose work changes the course of nations. But even in our smaller spheres, there's more than the fickle immediacy of our ministries. Sometimes, we'll spy glimpses of the long-horizon impacts of our humble work. The mother of a young person I taught and baptized years ago in another state emailed me recently to share her now college-aged daughter's excitement about her Bible class. She wrote in gratitude for my role in "making faith credible" to her kids. I can run for at least a week on a note like that. It took a decade to arrive.

My teenage sons and I hiked the Teton Crest Trail through the mountains of Wyoming. We pushed through forty miles of elevation, rain, and cold (wet tent, wet boots, and wet sleeping bags were not fun). But we caught some awesome vistas through the mists as we followed a trail that curled around boulders and scree fields and over glaciers half-eaten by summer. We crossed meadows thick with wildflowers. Marmots flashed their threatening grins. Challenging stretches of the route snaked through stones, and we had to consider and clamber and find a way.

Thus is ministry in the rural church. We can just see the promise of something ahead and above us, but there are boulders everywhere and we have to find a way. Or something like that. I know I'm pressing a glib, playdough metaphor onto the fearsome landscape that is the church. What we're longing for is success, and that, above all, cannot be guaranteed. But I'm convinced that the decisive ingredient of success isn't know-how or degrees or charisma. I think it's fortitude. It's persistence. Boulders, boulders everywhere, and all too often we give up. Or we settle for an unbalanced vision that prioritizes faithfulness to the exclusion of fruitfulness.

Maybe this is just one more guilt trip for perennially harried rural pastors. (I'm feeling a little guilty as I write this.) We all know that sometimes the puddle dries up even for the very best and most driven pastors. They're good at what they do. They're dedicated. They love God and other people. And things fall apart.

Yet I wonder whether success sometimes eludes us because for whatever reason (and there are many), we're unwilling to find a way. It could be hurt. It could be hopelessness. It could be frustration with the congregation or community. Maybe sometimes we fail to push through.

I've been there.

I suspect I've given up too easily and succumbed too readily to the loping logic of some half-nomadic, lupine urge to move on. I'm ambivalent about my history of ministry transitions. Sometimes I find myself standing there after a move, and a move, and another move, clutching a box of day-old reasons and wondering whether my heart was discerning or just devious above all else, as Jeremiah 17:9 puts it. Like everyone else, I've been acculturated to leave. I know I can't fully trust my instincts when it comes to moving on.

This isn't to say that keeping on is always right, pushing off ever a mistake. Discernment about when to move on will mean paying attention to the cues our souls are giving us and taking seriously that our hungers and hurts can be signs of God's leading. We'll need trusted people near us who can see and speak a greater truth over our lives than whatever welter of frustration and anxiety and neophilia is knotting inside us.

Sometimes, God calls us to something else, somewhere else. But question itchy feet.

In a reflection on the phenomenon of pastors giving up too soon, Eugene Peterson writes about spending days observing a kingfisher at a pond near his Montana home. Per Peterson, the bird dove thirty-seven times before it managed to catch a fish. Peterson adopted a kingfisher mindset. Whenever he heard from ministers who felt that they'd failed, that nothing seemed to work, he would ask winsomely, "How many times have you tried? Thirty-seven?" Peterson notes that this is not a recipe for implementing someone else's prepackaged approach. Pastors are not wrong to attend conferences or seek out leadership training. But so often they would ask, "What do you have to do to get a congregation?" "Forget it," writes Peterson. "Just be yourself and not anybody else. Just you."[13]

I'm attracted to Peterson's words, because I think push-through lands somewhere near the intersection of faithful persistence and being ourselves. At the risk of sounding like the side of a box of herbal tea: Be persistent and be yourself. Sometimes, just being persistent can become rote. And sometimes, just being oneself can lead to inertia. Authentic push-through challenges us to find a way, but while taking seriously the unique ways that God has wired us up. We bring ourselves—God-called, Christ-gifted, Spirit-sufficed—and seek and knock and try and (sometimes) fail. We find a way.

With all of this talk of persistence and push-through, we can risk turning into "tryhards," those trying to make a way by sheer effort and force of enthusiasm. That won't work either. It's joyless to be a tryhard—and as my teenage sons assure me, deeply uncool. All that panting, desperate effort runs contrary to the restful promises of Psalm 127, where God "gives sleep to his beloved." And it makes for a poor facsimile of the abundant life that Jesus offers. And in any case, what does it mean to "try"? Like failure, perhaps the concept of *trying* is a modern confection. We do something to achieve some end in the life of the church, and if it doesn't work like we imagined or envisioned—well, we *tried*. Trying implies that we have a handle on what it is we're doing, that we know what we're aiming for. In the rural church, I suspect that's scarcely the case. There are too many impossible realities to consider, and when we're truly responding to the Spirit's leading, our paths open onto vistas we couldn't have anticipated or even imagined achieving. Was Adoniram Judson *trying*? He went to Burma. He learned the language. He lost dear ones. He translated the Scriptures. Adoniram Judson did the work. That was it. But I'm not sure he would have said that he was trying. Perhaps it's time to quote Yoda's words to Luke Skywalker: "Do or not do. There is no try."[14]

Pastor Paul Richardson serves the small Missouri town of Licking.[15] When we spoke, Richardson recalled how after some six years of hard work, he was frustrated and ready to move on. His ministry in Licking had not developed as planned. Sure, he had notched up some wins. His congregation had been willing to experiment and make changes for the sake of effective outreach, and they had experienced modest growth. But Richardson felt stuck, suspicious that he was passing up better opportunities to serve elsewhere. Were it not for the God-timely intervention of an older pastor mentor, Richardson likely would have left. His mentor asked him, "Did you know that the Lord called you to Licking?" Yes, said Richardson. "Then you need to be equally assured that God is calling you to leave."

Something began to loosen in him, and an incredible transformation began to unfold. Pastor Richardson recommitted himself to serving his congregation. He re-covenanted with himself and God to become the very best pastor and leader he could to the congregation. He decided to let God take it from there. Richardson stayed put. In fact, Richardson considers "a firm commitment between yourself and God" to stay put to be "extremely vital" in moving rural congregations toward thriving.

In the few years after Richardson's recommitment, his congregation was able to purchase property and construct a modern building. They grew in all the important ways, including in numbers. In our conversation, Richardson reflected that had he failed to push through, if he had left when he was frustrated, he would have missed all the growth that God had planned for him and his congregation.

The apostle Paul writes in 2 Corinthians 4:11 that "while we live, we are always being given up to death for Jesus' sake, so that the life of Jesus may be made visible in our mortal flesh." Which tells us this: Our life and our death, success and failure and all that lies between, finds its meaning and purpose and grounding in the life of Christ. As Romans 14:8 declares, whether we succeed or whether we fail, whether we walk upon the water (or not), we are the Lord's. There are no dead ends— not truly, not ultimately. Everything can become grist for the mill of a life on the way with Christ. There will be moments when we will faithfully obey the word of the Lord to get into the boat. We'll paddle out with everything we've got. And then storms, storms, gobbling dark waves and punching winds and storms. Jesus will intend to pass us by, and then what?

Just this: His plans are his own, but they are good, because he is good.

And this: "Take heart, it is I; do not be afraid" (Mark 6:50).

6

Coming to the Cross

Jesus said, "If any want to become my followers, let them deny themselves and take up their cross and follow me."
—Mark 8:34

I met a young guy and his young family at a Mennonite jamboree one summer. They had just moved to the area, and (here's where my ears really perked up) they were looking for a church. I told him I was the pastor of a nearby congregation that they should consider visiting. He responded: "Tell me about your church. Sell it to me."

So I did. I set about trying to sell him on our church. Inside sales, right? How hard can it be? Though I must have been a crummy salesman, because they never did drop by to check us out.

Eugene Peterson observed that somewhere along the way, pastors exchanged the vocation of pastoring for that of shopkeeping. Pastors have become "preoccupied with shopkeeper's concerns—how to keep the customers happy, how to lure customers away from competitors down the street, how to package the goods so that the customers will lay out more money."[1] And there I was, slipping on my shopkeeper's hat and tying on my shopkeeper's apron, leaning in with my low shopkeeper's voice to win some new customers. *We have a fully-featured church with padded pews.*

The problem is not so much that I invited this young family to visit our church. That's the kind of thing pastors do: we welcome people, we evangelize, we pursue. The problem is that whatever my most honorable intentions—discipling, building up the congregation, cultivating capacity to reach the lost—another part of me wanted to see them in our church because they were mythical beasts something like unicorns: a young family with kids. I wanted to look out from my pulpit and see them and be confirmed in having done my job well. A part of me just wanted to count them.

Of course, this is the question in the rural church: What do we count? In many ways, it's the same question any congregation in any locale might face: What are our metrics for measuring progress and success? The question becomes more acute for rural congregations because of a number of factors, including limited population, in some cases even declining population, as well as the unique role that congregations play in rural communities. How does a church know when it's carrying out its mission truly and well? What are our measures for fruitfulness and faithfulness in the rural church?

In Mark 8, Jesus gets to the heart of what it means to follow him: "If any want to become my followers, let them deny themselves and take up their cross and follow me" (v. 34). This means at least two things. First, following Jesus has a particular cast. Not everything that we might wish to do in Jesus' name counts, as it were. Jesus said so himself in the Sermon on the Mount: "Not everyone who says to me, 'Lord, Lord,' will enter the kingdom of heaven, but only the one who does the will of my Father in heaven" (Matthew 7:21). Jesus has set a standard that we can measure ourselves against. Second, that standard is cruciform: "Take up [your] cross and follow me." Which is to say, the measure of all things in discipleship—as well as in ministry and the church—is the cross. The cross is the yardstick that gives us our metric for life in the church. We will measure our fruitfulness and faithfulness by the cross. Yet if the cross is our yardstick, it's an elusive yardstick, one that can read success both in the invisible prayer life of someone like the nineteenth-century desert hermit Charles de Foucauld and in the bustling suburban church, fecund with new disciples.

I'm convinced that though there are profound risks, it's possible to develop metrics that allow us to gauge fruitfulness and faithfulness in the rural church. But if they are not grounded in the cross, whatever metrics we might employ become merely shopkeeping.

DON'T LOSE ANYONE: THE RISK OF METRICS

The disposition to rural ministry tracks two lines: faithfulness and fruitfulness. Faithfulness reflects the church in its being. It's a factor of abiding. As Jesus said, "Abide in me as I abide in you" (John 15:4). The church doesn't have to accomplish anything in order to be faithful, and indeed, faithfulness is often secret and interior. John Calvin famously wrote: "Wherever we see the Word of God rightly preached and heard, and the sacraments administered according to Christ's institution, there, it is not to be doubted, a church of God exists."[2] A congregation might not be doing anything much beyond abiding in Christ and clinging to the ancient teaching and practice of the gospel, but in doing so it can excel at faithfulness. Faithfulness is largely intangible. Prayer, Scripture study, love for one another, and worship are marks of faithfulness.

Fruitfulness has to do with the church in its doing, as the church leans into the fullness of its mission. Fruitfulness is characterized by works of mercy. Jesus gave six of those works of mercy in Matthew 25:35–36: feed the hungry, give drink to the thirsty, clothe the naked, welcome the stranger, visit the sick, and visit the imprisoned. Christian tradition couldn't resist rounding out the list to the perfect number seven by adding "bury the dead."[3] In addition, we see fruitfulness in the spiritual works of mercy that were developed by medieval thinkers, especially Thomas Aquinas: counsel the doubtful, instruct the ignorant, admonish sinners, comfort the afflicted, forgive offenses willingly, bear wrongs patiently, pray.[4] The church is fruitful when it carries out the works of mercy.

Of course, associating faithfulness with being and fruitfulness with doing is overly simplistic. Ultimately, we're pursuing faithful doing and fruitful being. Jesus said: "Those who abide in me and I in them bear much fruit, because apart from me you can do nothing" (John 15:5). Abiding and doing are synergies, two sides of the same coin. Yet our tendency is to focus mainly on the fruitful doing. We ask questions of "How many?" and "How much?" We fixate on what church leadership and growth experts Ed Stetzer and Thom Rainer call the "the three Bs: bodies, budget, and buildings."[5] It's true that in one way, leaders need to measure something. We need some way of honestly assessing how things are going and tracking progress toward change. After all, as turnaround strategist Gil Rendle puts it, "A system gets what it measures. If we don't measure anything, we won't get anything."[6] Which is true enough in its way, but in the rural church our measurements often reinforce a perception of scarcity. One tiny little congregation I visited on the sparse plains of western Kansas had the standard-issue wooden sign at the front of the sanctuary. White plastic tiles with black numbers were slatted in to display the hymns and giving from last week—as well as the attendance: 10. Does displaying that number accomplish any work in the congregation? Or is it merely a metric of despair?

Part of what makes rural *rural* is its limited population. Measure all you want, but you're not going to count your way to a sea change in communities of one hundred or two hundred or five hundred. As Stetzer and Rainer aptly point out, "Churches below fifty in attendance can change drastically from year to year. So much so that it is nearly impossible to track and to create adequate statistical benchmarks."[7] A family moves in, a family moves out, and the stats jiggle like a trampoline. They just don't tell you much.

What's more, fostering growing congregations in communities experiencing net out-migration—as in some rural areas—is a tall order. "God is able from these stones to raise up children to Abraham" (Luke 3:8). Yet here we are with an empty nursery.

I know: Excuses, excuses.

But however much we might try to moralize their decline and abstract strategies for the future, the story of rural churches in North America is in so many ways just the story of population change due to economic opportunity and cultural trends toward smaller families. In any case, rural churches often have a history of tremendous numerical "success"—particularly in the 1950s through 1970s when the nursery was packed and you had three choirs to choose from. No longer.[8]

Furthermore, in our tiniest communities, the rural church plays a unique structural role. People are deeply interrelated. To belong to a family is to belong to a church—and vice versa (sort of). It's a momentous act to change churches or begin attending church for the first time. Whether implicitly or explicitly, rural communities often operate on a parish model: everyone connects to the local congregation, or to a handful of local congregations, whether they actively participate in church life or not. This is why church planting in rural communities can be perceived as deeply disruptive (and why it may also be deeply necessary, as we'll explore in the next chapter).

So should we do away with metrics altogether? No doubt many rural and small churches could use a breather from the temptations and anxieties of counting. But the reality is that rural churches do have metrics—and one in particular. Quite often, the primary metric of the rural church is neither fruitfulness nor faithfulness, but how well we hang on to everyone. It's the membership list doubling as the Lamb's book of life from Revelation 21:27. Don't lose anyone. On this metric, what counts the most is keeping everyone together. Growth from the outside is nice, but what we really want is the kids to come back after college and stand up front to present their babies for dedication or baptism. Continuity is key. Pastors and leaders walk the spider's web between multigenerational stakeholders. The life of the church often overlaps with economic life. This can be a positive testimony to the early church model of sharing and mutual aid and the whole of life being shaped by the gospel, but it can also get sticky when livelihood and church membership become too closely enmeshed. In highly agricultural communities, for instance, land use and transfer can get tied up in church affiliation. When we place hanging on to everyone at the center of everything, balance, outward conflict avoidance, and zero-sum preference-matching become key strategies.

I think we can do better. I'm convinced we can deploy life-giving, affirmative metrics that pair faithfulness and fruitfulness and that challenge congregations to move beyond stasis and preference toward a missional future.

There are still risks in this. Some metrics can be used to falsely ascribe value to leaders and congregations—as if numerical decline means poor pastoring or an uninspired congregation. We can engage in unhealthy comparison, which leads to envy, often wearing a disguise of constructive critique. We can fixate on scarcity. We can game the system by skimming off the top only numbers that paint a positive picture of our work.[9] Pastors in free church systems can all too easily fall into this trap, choosing to serve only congregations they regard as most likely to succeed and leaving the tough cases to struggle on their own. Perhaps worst of all, pastors and leaders can slip into an actuarial mindset. This sort of approach is dominated by stats, control, technique, and efficiency, mimicking the "scientific management" techniques developed by Frederick Wilson Taylor in the late nineteenth century.[10] When applied to congregations, it's the old refrain: Run the church like a business.

What scientific management risks missing is the essential sacredness of the church. Managerial approaches neglect the ways that the church can remain true to its essential one, holy, catholic, and apostolic nature whether it grows, fades, or plateaus. The church's most important activity—mainly, worship of the triune God—is extravagantly inefficient. It conspicuously produces no easily tallied results. So take off your grubby secular sandals—this place is holy ground. We only measure the church with fear and trembling. After all, the church belongs to Christ. It's his bride. But it's also his baby, and Christ has given the church everything it needs for life and godliness (2 Peter 1:3). Whatever else happens, this is enough.

ONE NEW PERSON: TOWARD AN AUTHENTIC METRIC FOR THE RURAL CHURCH

What metrics do we bring to the life of the rural church? Counting alone won't get us where we need to go, and it may even lead us into temptation and sin by generating pride and a reliance on our own efforts. Or we slip into shame and resignation and disdain. King David made the mistake of relying on his own efforts when he sought a census of the fighting men of Israel in 2 Samuel 24. The numbers filtered back to him where he calculated from his iron throne, hash marks lined up like swords. Muscle tabulated by tribe, clan, and family—enough to be strong and secure. Perhaps enough not to fear. Not even the Lord. That was the temptation. And when David came to his senses (at God's terrifying prompting), he relented.

But might a careful metric at least help leaders assess the well-being of the congregation they serve? My sense is that most of us don't need numbers to know whether our church is thriving. Numbers often stand in for intuition and attempt to substitute with a dashboard what can only be learned through years spent with a people in a place. And numbers just can't do justice to the diverse contexts of rural congregations. We need something that takes stock of the church in a way that at least nods to what Colossians 3:3 describes as the hidden life of the church with Christ in God.

Any measure of the church must be appropriate and contextual. A congregation of thirty in an isolated rural community of seventy faces challenges and holds promises that are worlds away from a small church in a growing suburb. Our measurements should be life-giving and affirming. The tool here is to listen like Mary, treasuring the story of our congregation in our heart (Luke 2:19). And it seems to me that we need to be realistic, but also daring. Numerical growth

in many small rural congregations might not garner denominational plaudits. Pastor Tim Koch, whom I mentioned in
the last chapter, told me that his goal for a congregation he
once served was to add one new person a year.[11] That's it.
The one new person could even be a baby born into their
congregation. In a town of eighty-something, one new person
is not a bad growth target.

Above all, we don't want our metrics to discount God's
power to transform people and community and congregation.
There should be some hunger built into the metrics, a longing for more than we can ask or imagine. Our metrics should
be realistic yet calibrated to the impossible. We need something that considers faithfulness—love for God, beautiful and
engaging worship, intelligent sermons, lives rich with works
of mercy, and so forth. And we need measures of fruitfulness:
are we inviting, are new people showing up, are we serving the
world and the neighborhood?

THE LITTLE MULBERRY RULE

Perhaps what we're looking for is less a metric than a rule.

In the ancient church, a rule was a set of commitments made
by a monastic community. The rule was their words to live by,
the standard for their way of life. Benedict of Nursia created
what became one of the most influential and enduring rules:
the Rule of Saint Benedict. There were other rules both before
and after Benedict's. In the Eastern church, Basil's rule took
pride of place. Augustine in North Africa had an unsystematic
collection of precepts that guided the community where he lived
during his days as bishop of Hippo. But Benedict's rule stands
out for its clarity, comprehensiveness, and wisdom. Benedict
covered everyday challenges like the adequacy of monks' robes
and ensuring sufficient food—many early monasteries prided

themselves on overly austere fasting that harmed the health of the monks. But the power of Benedict's Rule is its spiritual heart. In chapter 4, Benedict lays out what he calls the "tools of the spiritual craft." It begins with Jesus' greatest commandments—loving God and neighbor—continues through the Ten Commandments, and calls the monks to follow Christ with their whole lives through renunciation, prayer, and kindness. "Never turn away . . . when someone needs your love," writes Benedict. "Pray for your enemies out of love of Christ. . . . Day by day remind yourself that you are going to die."[12]

Benedict called his masterpiece a "little rule," and I think that's what we need too: a rule—just a little one—that can help us take stock of our labor in the rural church.[13]

According to author and practical ministry entrepreneur Andy Crouch, the concept of Benedict's Rule grew from the Latin word *regula*, which implied not only "regulation" but "trellis"—like for supporting a growing grapevine. Crouch calls a rule a "set of practices to guard our habits and guide our lives."[14] Author Stephen Macchia writes that a rule "articulates our intentions and identifies the ways in which we want to live." A *regula* is not "something fixed and rigid," but "something to hang on to in the dark."[15]

Crouch and Macchia tap the concept of a rule as a way for individuals to order their lives toward Christ in a holistic and intentional way. But it strikes me that rural congregations can benefit from a rule as well. A rule is forward-looking, centering, and generative. There's no one way to live it out, and yet a rule calls for an act of imagination.

There are places in the Gospels where Jesus calls us to imagine the impossible. He speaks of small and unassuming things which contain within them grains of impossible turnaround. It's the wheat that dies and "bears much fruit" (John 12:24).

It's the mustard seed sign of the kingdom which, "when sown upon the ground, is the smallest of all the seeds on earth," but becomes so good and growing that all kinds of birds take refuge in it (Mark 4:31–32). That same mustard seed becomes an icon of faith: "If you had faith the size of a mustard seed, you could say to this mulberry tree, 'Be uprooted and planted in the sea,' and it would obey you" (Luke 17:6).

In a basic sense, biblical faith is entrusting ourselves to God's goodness. But faith is also about making space for the impossible—being able to fling a mulberry tree into the heart of the sea with a word. That just doesn't happen. Faith, in this sense, involves the imagination. The question of faith is: Can we imagine such a thing? Does our field of vision, our concept of what is possible and real and good and beautiful, align with Jesus' view? Is our mindset shaped by the mind of Christ? This is part of what Paul is talking about in Romans 12:2: "Do not be conformed to this world, but be transformed by the renewing of your minds." In other words, let your imagination, your view of what is possible, be shaped by Jesus.

The Gospels offer another version of this lesson where Jesus says that with mustard seed faith we can move a mountain into the heart of the sea. But I like mulberries. I think the mulberry tree might be the perfect image of the rural church.

Check your commentaries and you'll learn that the mulberry Jesus was talking about in Luke 17 was the *Morus nigra*—the black mulberry, common in the Near East and the Mediterranean. In North America, we have the *Morus rubra*—the red mulberry.[16] But they're really similar. Both produce little purplish fruit that resembles a blackberry that people and birds alike love. And they both have weedlike characteristics.

The mulberry is ubiquitous in North America. The internet says mulberry trees grow in every state except Nevada (I don't believe it. I bet you could find a mulberry somewhere in Nevada). My family loves mulberries. We make jam. We eat them raw. We bake a mean mulberry rhubarb pie. But the thing about the mulberry is that it grows everywhere, and it grows fast. We harvest our mulberries from a couple of spots in the park. But in my backyard, I'm constantly doing battle with mulberries, cutting them out from the fencerow and the chicken run and the raspberry trellis.

In that way, the mulberry is sort of the quintessential rural tree. It grows in marginal places, on the edge of things, wherever it can get a roothold. It's a scrappy tree. In rural communities, wherever there's a ragged and wild place, you find mulberries. Mulberries may be akin to a weed, but they're a weed that gives wonderful fruit.

In our impossible time, I think God is calling forth a reformation of the imagination among rural and small-town leaders. God is calling us to imagine something more, to imagine that we can do much, that there is a future threading through the rocks and the flinty hard places. It's a mulberry sort of vision. And I'm convinced that one way we embody that vision is like what we see in the Scriptures and the ancient church: not a series of metrics focused on what's at hand and countable, but through a hopeful posture that sizes up faithfulness and fruitfulness both. It's a mulberry metric. Or maybe, with an ever-so-slight twist of the imagination we can graft in the apostle Paul's signs of Spirit-filled fruitfulness from Galatians 5:22–23 (CEB):

The Little Mulberry Rule

1. Love—Love God and neighbor.
2. Joy—Worship the triune God in the beauty of holiness.
3. Peace—Pray.

4. Patience—Create space for Christ to grow in us over the long term.
5. Kindness—Live mercifully.
6. Goodness—Engage the neighborhood with the goodness of the gospel.
7. Faithfulness—Talk to people about Jesus, and encourage and equip the congregation for outreach.
8. Gentleness—Serve, especially the school and the poor, and the world through mission.
9. Self-control—Be authentic in your place.

"Against such things there is no law," writes Paul (v. 23 NIV). But they are a kind of rule.

There's nothing particularly rural about the shaping of these commitments, and I think that's a strength. Doing rural ministry truly and well should, in a lot of ways, just look like doing ministry truly and well. Yet each of these commitments is open to a uniquely rural bent. For instance, rural ministry is animated by a commitment to prayer and holds the potential for outsized influence in the community. Rural congregations need to be reminded of their connection to the global church—and their agency to make an impact through mission and service. What's more, any congregation in any community, no matter how small or isolated, can live out this little rule. Mulberries grow everywhere.

These are the kinds of things that I've discovered thriving rural churches do. They arrive here through trial and error and the Holy Spirit. Like number 3: pray. Every thriving rural church is a praying church. There are the women who meet before worship to lift up the service, or the intentional times of congregational prayer and fasting, or the pastor who devotes a day a week to prayer. Thriving rural churches I've met are deeply involved in and relevant to their community. Thriving rural churches find creative ways to talk to people about Jesus. And so on.

There's always more we could say. The Little Mulberry Rule is a starting place. The best way to evaluate a congregation or ministry according to this rule may be to take a contemplative approach. Sit with it. Dialogue in a small group of leaders.

If you need numbers, consider a congregational Apgar test, as proposed by Gil Rendle.[17] Apgar is a series of five categories that healthcare providers check to judge a baby's health immediately upon birth and then five minutes afterward. In each category—for instance pulse or respiration—the baby is given a ranking of 0, 1, or 2. Total scores of 7, 8, or 9 mean the baby is doing well and in good health. Lower scores prompt extra attention and action. When our youngest son squeezed into the world after a couple of stressful months of this and that, the pediatric nurse evaluated him as an 8. It was the first score of his life, and I was ready to go all tiger dad and advocate for him. *An 8? Are you kidding? Look at how beautiful he is! Admit it: he's the most perfect child ever born in this hospital. Totally a 10.* But I bit my lip.

Perhaps each member of your leadership team could measure your congregation by giving a 0, 1, or 2 for each line of the rule. Areas with lower collective scores merit extra attention and action. Higher scores call for gratitude.

So there you have it: The Little Mulberry Rule, nine commitments for thriving rural and small-town churches. Do these things and ye shall live.

THE HIDDEN LIFE OF THE CHURCH

Yet let us not overestimate the humble mulberry tree. The Little Mulberry Rule isn't a guarantee of rural church success.

There's no such thing. The Little Rule is formative. It externalizes the inner compass of the rural leader for the whole of the church. The Little Rule points to a way of living the Christian walk in the rural neighborhood. It begins the journey and gives us some signposts to check in on how we're faring. But that's it.

Doing these things will never amount to doing the one thing needful, because in the end what we most need to do is not a thing. It's a relationship. It's following Jesus. And it's following him by taking up our cross. Doing so is no guarantee of our success—even the success of the church—but rather is to relinquish all to follow Christ.

In 1966, Thomas Merton wrote in a letter to peace activists: "You may have to face the fact that your work will be apparently worthless and even achieve no result at all." He continued: "As you get used to this idea you start more and more to concentrate not on the results but on the value, the rightness, the truth of the work itself."[18]

The life of the church, like the life of the individual believer, always remains partly "hidden with Christ in God" (Colossians 3:3). We'll never know the whole of our fruitfulness—at least not until the Last Day. "There is nothing hidden, except to be disclosed; nor is anything secret, except to come to light," says Mark 4:22. To follow Jesus in the rural church is to give up any claim to be able to guarantee or measure our ultimate effectiveness. It's to surrender to the Lord who calls us to hard and sparse places and to embrace the promise that "in the Lord [our] labor is not in vain" (1 Corinthians 15:58).

The measure of all things is the cross, which is to say that the final metric for our faithfulness and fruitfulness will be grounded in the suffering heart of God. Faithfulness and fruitfulness will be carried out by God's means, toward God's ends, in marvelous ways known only to God. There will always be a hiddenness to the life of the disciple and the church. That hidden life with God is the beginning and end of rural ministry.

Which is why the cross must always stand as the measure of all life in the church. The cross speaks to God's abundant love and grace demonstrated in thriving, bustling, growing congregations—rural or otherwise. But the cross also reminds us that *more* and *bigger* (even the Christian versions of *more* and *bigger*) never exhaust God's kingdom mission.

The way of the cross attests to the mystery of God's power made manifest in smallness and renunciation. There have always been Christians down through the ages who have understood this. They have seen their mission not in straightforwardly countable outward accomplishments, but in silence and hiddenness. They've been people like the fourth-century contemplatives who abandoned careers and standing in the cities to pursue God in the deserts of Egypt. In fact, the desert has often figured prominently in the vocation of those who seek God in smallness and renunciation.

In the late nineteenth century, Charles de Foucauld, a playboy-soldier-turned-desert-prayer-warrior, left his family fortune to his sister and eventually made his way into the deserts of French-controlled Algeria to dwell in an isolated place among the Tuareg people.[19] Foucauld prayed. He showed hospitality to all comers. He testified to the way of Jesus among a predominantly Muslim people. But despite his desire to found a monastic community, he could not persuade others to join him. Writes poet and Foucauld biographer Bonnie Thurston, "For fifteen years, Foucauld was a missionary priest who converted nobody."[20] Even his death left an ambiguous legacy. Was he martyred for his Christian faith? Or simply murdered in a botched robbery?

And while the life of some individuals, like that of Adoniram Judson, bears unequivocal fruit after death, Foucauld's legacy is more modest—at least by outward measures. He did not convert nations. Still, two religious orders dedicated to "littleness and gentleness" grew from his example and life: the Little Brothers of Jesus and the Little Sisters of Jesus.[21]

What do we make of this? Foucauld's life contains a completeness and truth that cannot be written off for lack of outward success. He succeeded brilliantly in becoming nothing for the sake of Christ. In fact, Foucauld's greatest legacy may be a single prayer, known as the "Prayer of Abandonment," which begins: "My Father, I abandon myself to you. Make of me what you will. Whatever you make of me, I thank you. I am ready for everything. I accept everything."[22]

Can we do anything less in the sometimes deserts of rural places? Whatever success by whatever measures, we belong to Christ, and it's his self-giving life that forms us. This is precisely what we're getting at when we claim the cross as the measure of our lives: Christ before us, Christ behind us, Christ through and through.

7

Resurrection Happens

Go, tell his disciples and Peter that he is going ahead of you to Galilee. —Mark 16:7

On a cold January day after a prairie blizzard, I slid our car off the road.

My wife and I and infant firstborn son had an appointment with the pediatrician. Snow caked the pavement, and the smart money would have been on canceling the appointment and staying inside. But why be smart when you can be in a hurry? I took the backcountry route to cut time and thereby set in motion a series of unfortunate events involving a partially plowed road, a lazy four-wheeled pirouette, and a marshmallow drift that glommed on to our family sedan and wouldn't let go. We were stuck. Were it not for a kindly man with a large truck and a tow strap, we would have stayed that way. And we missed our appointment with the pediatrician.

In my experience, perhaps the greatest fear of rural pastors is getting stuck. We fear getting stuck in the seeming motionlessness of rural communities and congregations. We fear getting stuck by missing out and being left behind. Something inside us sinks (even though we know it shouldn't) when we

119

look out at our white-crowned congregation that we're able to serve only by making ends meet by substitute teaching or insurance hustling or driving school buses. And you may ask yourself, "Where does that highway go to?" To be a rural pastor is to face the Fear of the Dead End.

The Fear of the Dead End works as a metaphor because it's a rural reality first. Swing into leafy Old Town of your nearest city, and there we call the dead end a cul-de-sac. It's a haute dead end that reflects tranquility, the prestige of being out of the way. But there are honest-to-God dead ends in rural places. The road forks, one branch bounding for the infinite horizon while its dirt road sister coils over the hill and ends in a puddle of red mud.

The Fear of the Dead End may be a particularly North American phenomenon, or at least, it may play out in a particular way in North America. Not long ago, I read the description of a village in the deep rural countryside of France. The road to town "leads to nowhere else." There is no "café, no shop, no post office, no boulangerie. Nobody passes through it by chance or even design."[1] Yet the description of this little village with its ancient hilltop chapel and absent priest watercolors my imagination something picturesque. They farm apricots and eat tapenade smeared over baguettes. Outside, the cicadas are singing in raspy French.

Rural North American communities are somehow different. It's not for lack of beauty. It's all God's country, if you have trained yourself to look. But we occupy the squares that track the dirt roads differently. Maybe it's because most of us—with the exception of Indigenous peoples—haven't been here that long. We're from every continent but this one. Maybe we stand on the soil differently because long before the assertion that this land is your land and my land, it was home to other peoples, peoples who have occupied it for thousands of years. We still do not know how to reckon with this history or what it means for living on this land today.

Or maybe we inhabit the space differently because America is an idea before it's a place. Thus our relationship with land and place sometimes becomes one of function rather than identity.

This is why we fear the Dead End: not because it challenges our personal geography or aesthetic, but because it picks at the threads of our identity, an identity wrapped up in our participation in the great culture-making engines of North America, which—like it or believe it or accept it or not—are in large part urban. To go rural—really rural, the little dirt road places your GPS fears to tread—is to step outside of something.

Our culture's rapid and tectonic shifting around has crossbred with the ancient idea that "rural" is an outmoded category. It's the idea that *civilization* equates with *urbanization*, and that as people move to the city, rural will at some point simply cease to exist in a meaningful way. I've read breathless articles claiming that farming on the Great Plains is increasingly handled by drones because nobody lives out there anymore. It's "flyover territory" to the nth degree. In our cultural imaginary, rural becomes an uninhabitable place.

Or maybe internet culture has melted rural cultures. All those scrolling reels mean everybody's in line at the same water fountain. In the social diffusion of our moment, all places become no place in particular. And when the local gets gobbled up, it's urban that prevails.

All of this is to say that our world pressures us to believe that to be someone you have to go somewhere, and that imagined somewhere probably has a downtown and good coffee and an IKEA. It's probably not rural.

Yet I'm convinced that in the ways that matter most, rural places are open to the goodness and grace of God. They're places worthy of our fullest love and respect. God made them. God loves them. And I'm convinced that the great work of our age isn't just drawing attention to the plight and promise of rural, but to speak with enduring affection of how life in the sticks can be rich and full and authentic, if in different ways than in the cities or suburbs. I think the work of our times will involve challenging the notion that the path to rural is a path to nowhere: a Dead End.

What I'm getting at is bigger than taking rural seriously. It's more about how we approach life. What does a faithful life path look like? Following Jesus doesn't mean making all the winning decisions and avoiding dead ends. Sometimes we need the dead ends, the unpaved roads, the backcountry. And sometimes, those places need us.

Of course, this willingness to walk the dead ends is only possible when we cultivate a bold hope in the resurrection. Calling something a "dead end" is more than a metaphor. A thread traces from all the clenching ways we can feel stuck to death with its huge and monosyllabic vastness that reduces to nothingness. Every time we hit the wall, we're banging up against death.

In the first verses of Mark 16, the women bang up against death at the tomb, conscious of all that stands in the way of their completing their task and mission. "Who will roll away the stone for us?" they ask (v. 3). Their only words in Mark's resurrection account are those: a coolly rational assessment of the state of their ministry. It's blocked. They're stuck. Even the appearance of the "young man" angelic figure doesn't elicit words from them. The women are "seized" by "terror and amazement," cotton-mouthed with death's hangover (v. 8). Most biblical scholars understand the original gospel text to end at verse 8 with the women's fear and trembling. If that's the case, then the last major word of the gospel is "afraid."

However, the gospel does not end with fear. The women are captured in their fearful, silent stuckness. But that's only temporary because they've been ordered back to Galilee. "He has been raised; he is not here," says the angel. "Go, tell his disciples and Peter that he is going ahead of you to Galilee" (vv. 6–7). Yes, remaining at the tomb is stuckness and fear and death. I suppose they could choose to stand there forever, a black-and-white snapshot in anguished lines. Yet there's hope: a return to Galilee, the place of mission in the gospel, and now in the full-color hope of the resurrection.

And here we are. So many of us in the rural church—so many pastors, so many leaders, all of God's people together— are standing with Mary and Mary and Salome. So many in the rural church feel stuck. We may want to chalk it up to COVID-19, but the global pandemic is only the latest factor in a two-century squeeze on the rural church. It was all there before, or at least, so much of it was. The pandemic years merely accelerated and revealed the profound challenges that rural congregations were already facing. But you know all this. You lived it too. We're all stuck now.

But here's the thing: stuckness is an imaginative posture. Stuckness snares our brains. We're stuck because we think stuck. I don't mean that we can just buck up and shake it off. We can't—at least, not on our own power. But the circumstances of our ministerial context don't in and of themselves determine whether we're stuck. Stuck is as stuck believes.

Take the women at the tomb. Their imaginations were captive to the theretofore perfectly compelling logic of death. Sure, Elijah resurrected a boy. Elisha too. Yes, there was the widow's son at Nain. There was Lazarus.[2] But that was then and this is now and dead is dead. The physician, it would seem, could not heal himself.[3] Their imaginations were stuck idling on dead.

Until.

The unimaginable and incomprehensible happened. See here: the tomb is bare. A cloth here and a cloth there are all that remain, unhurriedly folded in a tell of power.[4] Jesus has all the time in the world. Breaking the bars of Death is no reason not to make the bed. And this new set of facts on the ground shifted something within the women. Mark doesn't relay the shift. That may be the genius of his writing. The shift happens *after* we finish reading the gospel. We know the shift happened for the women because there's a *we* to read it at all. Mark 16:8 reports that the women "fled from the tomb," but their flight became a mission became a proclamation. They did not remain silent forever; they told the male disciples who told others and so on and go forth to make disciples of all nations. Those words—"He has been raised; he is not here" (v. 6)—were words of unsticking. They marked the moment when the women could begin to imagine another world. That was when resurrection came to infect their imagination.

Because if resurrection is possible, well, then that stirs things up a bit. Why not believe an ax head can float and the sun can hover overlong in the sky and a donkey can speak?[5] Resurrection becomes the defining fact of Christian existence. If Christ's body—pale, pierced, laid out with Nicodemus's reverence in the Arimathean's tomb—can shudder and breathe and Live, then what else?

ABIDE IN PLACE

When we first moved to central Kansas, I set about planting things. I grew up on a farm, and my dad likes to joke that I've got a little dirt in my shoes—wherever I go, I've got to put something in the ground and watch it take root. So when we went from having essentially no earth to work in Cusco, Peru, to having a big back yard with plenty of Kansas sun, I could barely contain myself. Spring hit, and I immediately planted asparagus and a grapevine. When I told a pastoral colleague at another local church what I was doing, she was surprised that I would plant things that take years to develop and bear fruit. It puzzled me, and she explained, "I just wouldn't be sure I was going to stay long enough."

Here's the situation as I see it. It's hard to stay put in rural communities. Maybe it's impossible. In one way, it's a geographical challenge. If we're married, work for our spouses is often distant or difficult to come by. If we have kids, they have to play all the sports. There's no robotics program to challenge our brightest. Internet is spotty. Maybe there's no restaurant or grocery store or—God forbid—Dollar General. A pastor in eastern Colorado told me that when the pandemic hit and his congregation sought to transition to online, they faced two hurdles. The first was that in their tiny rural church, they didn't have stable electrical current. The second was that they couldn't get internet installed with enough bandwidth to livestream. They tried to convince somebody to drive out from Denver to install it, but the installer kept making excuses and putting them off. Of course, not all rural communities deal with that sort of scarcity—including my own, which happens to have high-speed fiber-optic broadband internet, a great school, tons of work, and a swimming pool and pickleball courts just down the block from us.

But it's not just geography. Rural congregations and communities will often push us away. In part, it has to do with a rural community's deep structure. Who's on the inside of that architecture? Who gets a seat at the table?

In another way, it has to do with the special difficulties of process in rural congregations. Many rural congregations are designed for maximum input, perhaps because pastoral leadership over the long term has often proven transitory and scarce. They have a built-in tendency toward inertia. It's hard to make changes. They hold congregational votes on everything. So what hope is there?

But the resurrection gives us a bold hope to abide in place. This is why we go to the bedraggled congregations in the tough spots and we have the courage to stay there for a while and keep at it. That's easier said than done because struggling congregations are struggling for a reason—usually lots of reasons. They're all unhappy in their own way. And the pastor coming in from outside can't fix it—at least not quickly, and definitely not alone. Without hope for resurrection, we don't have much to go on.

No doubt this explains the trend among many rural church movers and shakers—particularly in the evangelical world—to write off historic churches in rural communities as lost causes. They have their reasons: doctrinal slide, loss of vitality, failure to engage the community. Those are not bad reasons. But in my experience, a whole lot of rural congregations are muddling along somewhere in the middle. Sure, they have their quirks and limitations. There are immovable objects strewn all across their congregational life. But historic congregations also have their glimmers of grace. And they can learn new tricks.

This is why it's especially important that the hope of resurrection is embedded in a whole way of life. Our resurrection hope comes to imprint a settled character. It's a way of being, not a fleeting feeling. This settled hope of resurrection is what allows us to pick the tough spots and go there. We make our homes between the rocks and the hard places.

What makes this challenging is not solely congregation and context. Someone from another congregation once pulled me aside and said, "We just make it so hard for you pastors, don't we?" To which I responded, "No! Not at all!" (Okay, maybe sometimes). But I think it's not (only) the people or the place that sometimes makes it hard. It's the husky little whisper behind the ear of every rural pastor saying *You could do better! You could succeed if you were somewhere else!*

There's only one way to resist the wicked temptation to seek our ministerial fortunes elsewhere, and that's to abide. As John 15:1–5 reports, Jesus said, "Abide in me as I abide in you." He said, "Apart from me you can do nothing." He said that if we're truly abiding in him, we'll "bear much fruit." To abide is to grow in a stability of character that's rooted in the incarnation. It's having the wherewithal to stick to it and stay put. But abiding is more than sticktoitiveness and remaining. It's really about growing into the kind of character that's able to stay present and engaged in discomfort and uncertainty and lean into the F5 shear forces of rural ministry. You'll know you're beginning to abide when you don't jump ship at the first opportunity to get out—or bail when you dent your sense of self on the first immovable object. Stability is learning to stand at that tension point where faithfulness becomes painful.

Saint Benedict, whose not-so-insignificant rule offers stunning clarity and wisdom for a life of faith, knew that practicing stability would be both the key to soul-craft and the great impossibility of lived community. Anglican theologian Rowan Williams writes that the Rule of Saint Benedict is "all about staying in the same place, with the same people. The height of self-denial, the extreme of asceticism, is not hair shirts and all-night vigils; it's standing next to the same person quietly for years on end."[6]

In the generation that followed Benedict, Gregory the Great—pope, pastor, saint—wrote a book called the *Life and Miracles of St. Benedict*. In Gregory's loving depiction, we read that Benedict spent much time in the wilderness as a hermit. After he had written his Rule, a group of wannabe monks invited him to serve as the head of their monastery and spiritual father. Writing a rule that would govern monasteries was Benedict's life work, so when this little rural congregation called the renowned holy man to be their pastor, Benedict sensed an opportunity to put into practice the convictions that he had developed. The monks deeply appreciated his teaching and leadership.

Until they didn't. The story goes that some monks slipped poison into Benedict's wine. When the time came for Benedict to stand and offer the customary blessing over the cup, he made the sign of the cross over the wine and the cup miraculously shattered, spilling the wine. God revealed to Benedict what they had done, and being a saint in the making, Benedict forgave them. But he also left.

Even a brush with poison couldn't knock the idea of community out of Benedict, and he would go on to gather and serve other monastic communities. Benedict was not some imaginary person with a flat halo, but a real human being who struggled with the same sorts of interpersonal chaff that we do today. Yet he never gave up on the long-term, strenuous work of being together in Christian community.

You've probably figured out that I think there's some correspondence between monasteries and rural communities when it comes to the challenge of living in close proximity to one another for long periods of time. This is one of the reasons I'm drawn to the Rule of Saint Benedict. Benedict realized that we need each other. We need community. But it's exactly at that place of becoming a community that we experience some of our biggest challenges. The place of fusion is also the place of fission. We can't live with community, and we can't live without it.

Sometimes we call it the "fishbowl effect," the way our lives are on display in the whole community. Anyone can face this reality in rural places, but pastors and families living pedestaled lives can experience special scrutiny. I talked to a pastor who said that part of his own process of maturation was getting to the place where he could sit on his front porch in his tiny little town and have a beer. (I still can't quite swing that). When I got called to my first pastorate in Washington, somebody trying to be helpful said that the community "could use a model family." Which (ahem), we are not. That kind of visibility is something we have to learn to manage in rural communities. Some never do. The visibility eats them alive.

But the work of abiding is more than just staying put through community's bumps and blessings. It's about making the imaginative, resurrectional shift that allows us to see how God is working in and through a place. Jesus has gone ahead of us into Galilee, and we have to learn to think resurrection.

Galilee is a concrete place, inside history. Go there. Be there. And not only that, Galilee is the place where so much of Jesus' ministry was lived out. He proclaimed the good news in Galilee and cast out demons in Galilee and called those first disciples by the seaside in Galilee.[7] Jesus turned water into wine in Galilee and healed multitudes in Capernaum of Galilee.[8] Acts 1:11 reports that his disciples were "men of Galilee." So when Jesus promised—and the angel reiterated—that he would meet the disciples in Galilee after he was raised, he was promising to meet them in the dailiness and ordinariness of their lives and transform that place into a place of mission.⁹ The resurrected Jesus didn't so much send the disciples out as *in*. He called them back to the places they knew.

There would be more to the mission. There would be others—most notably fervent Paul, that Pharisee caught up in God's extravagant grace—who would go out and out and beyond, setting his sights on the most distant horizon he could imagine: Spain.¹⁰ But for now Jesus was calling them back to themselves, to their hometowns and their old work. Was it a letdown? They had been off on God's errand, sleeping rough and living on prayers and borrowed bread. The things they had seen! And now? *Go back to Galilee.* What of Jerusalem? What of the world? You will see. But for now: Jesus "is going ahead of you to Galilee" (Mark 16:7).

To go to Galilee is to abide in place. It requires patient daring to go to Galilee, because Galilee doesn't fit the usual narrative of the transformational leader marching off to the exotic locale. Galilee is conspicuously not Jerusalem. It's relatively small. It's mostly rural. Galilee was the place where the disciples had their homes and work. Peter was the first to get it: "I am going fishing," he said after the resurrection (John 21:3). And it was there, amid the ordinary work and life of Galilee, that they encountered the resurrected Christ (v. 7).

We tend to define transformational leadership as goal-driven, as leadership that's always envisioning the Next Big Thing. I aspire to that sort of leadership every other Wednesday. The transformational rural pastor has a sort of mythology. A man (yes, it's usually a man) hears a call from God to leave the strip mall comforts of the suburbs and go rural to plant a new church. He overcomes adversity and sideways glances from the windows of old pickup trucks to launch a thriving congregation. All's well that ends well.

Except when does it end? Rural churches develop their multilayered organization structures and strong local leadership because rural communities have so often been subjected to the vagaries of boom-and-bust cycles—economically, but also demographically and spiritually. Pastors come and go. The people remain. What will that thriving rural church look like in twenty-five or fifty years? A more cynical person might say: Talk to me when you've crossed the century mark.

What I've discovered is that the rural church requires leadership that is willing to go and abide in Galilee. The Galilees of North America are out-of-the-way little hinter-places that need pastors to come and preach and baptize and feed them on the bread of life. Marry their smiling couples. Bless and bury their dead. Yes, think mission. Evangelize. Never settle. But—and this is the thing, the key, central, all-important thing—minister from Christ's resurrection power in the place as it is. This is not to get stuck and wind up at a dead end. It's to abide. That's what it means to go to Galilee. And that, it seems to me, is enough.

Galilee is flung ten thousand ways across rural North America by accident of train tracks and wagon trails and fresh-water springs. Where's your Galilee? Where is Jesus, like he did for the man from Gerasa, telling you to "return to your home, and declare how much God has done for you" (Luke 8:39)?

Pastor Jacob Bobby is a Lutheran pastor in Bloomfield, Nebraska. We spoke about how in his context, it's not the highly caffeinated church programs that gain traction in the community. Rather, it's the "meat and potatoes" ministry of preaching a good sermon, visiting the sick, and being available for funerals. Rev. Bobby understands his congregation to be thriving when (in a wonderfully Lutheran formulation) Word and Sacrament make a difference in people's lives. He's deeply involved in the community and committed to longevity, both factors that he is convinced lay the groundwork for effective ministry. He serves on the board of the local nursing home and performs funerals for families who don't have a church. Some evenings, you can find him in the local bar shooting pool (Lutherans can get away with this sort of thing), a practice that has given him an in with the guys and that has led to his performing a half-dozen weddings. Pastor Bobby wrangled one man into showing up at church by challenging him to a game of pool. If he beat him at pool, the man had to come. "Luckily," Pastor Bobby confided, "I'm way better than him."[11]

One line in Saint Benedict's Rule has long stood out to me. It's the last of his "tools for the spiritual craft": "Never lose hope in God's mercy."[12]

It seems to me that in the end, that's precisely what abiding is: Never giving up on God's resurrection mercy for people, for congregation, for community. It's going into a community and staying put not because we don't have a big enough vision or a strong enough drive or are looking to lead a quiet life in some imagined rural idyll, but because we never lose hope in God's mercy.

This may be the hardest thing of all. When you feel stuck, what is mercy? Where is it? For whom? On whose timeline? Poet Nate Klug calls mercy "water-torture-slow."[13] That seems about right. But like water itself, mercy is also incessant. It rounds every corner, erodes every impossible hardness. In the Christian life, we get enough of a taste of that liquid resurrection to believe it. Stay put long enough and you'll see it.

A marriage revives. A life—suddenly, unexpectedly—turns around. Every once in a while, you beat some guy at a game of pool and he shows up at church and hears the gospel. All of that on some square of plains or at a knot in the anonymous gravel road beyond the twist in the valley or along a cold-stone coast—our little snatch of Galilee that the resurrected Christ insists on loving and living in.

PLANT

I stand at winter's heart burying one of our elder saints. I position myself strategically next to the casket and lean into the wind, which ruffles my coat like crow feathers and thumps the canvas tent flaps. I speak funereal words proclaiming our hope in the resurrection printed on cardstock and battened down with clips. The Kansas prairie shows no mercy to soft preachers unprepared for the wind. *Dust to dust. Ashes to ashes.* The gears whimper as we lower the casket into the earth. It's the thud at the bottom that gets you.

The church is composed of "saints below and saints above / the church in earth and heav'n," as hymnwriter Charles Wesley put it.[14] At that point, my little congregation had more saints above than below. The cemetery far outstripped the sanctuary. I suppose that's what you expect after 130 years of being church in a place. But it's also the result of a fat century of imagining community as a big Mennonite *us* with little reason to ask about the new neighbors who've moved in.

We're not alone. Broad swathes of North America were resettled by Europeans who arrived in clumps from the Old Country—Germans, Swedes, Dutch, Spanish—and brought their religion with them: Mennonite and Lutheran and Reformed and Catholic. Of course, there are many more groups, waves of people settling in colonies that they crafted to look and taste and sound like home. This is in addition to the rich customs and faith traditions of African peoples and others brought by force to the so-called New World. The rural communities that immigrants and others founded were spannered by marriage and common language and intricate ethnic customs. People are bound together across generations.

That's the *structure* of the community, the matrix of relationships that hold the community together and give it a sense of identity and internal integrity. This structure is the outworking of a rural community's ongoing conversation about its identity. Who are we? Who belongs? How does power flow within the community? Who will associate with who? (And who won't?) What makes us, us?

The structure is "I know a guy" writ into every aspect of life. In my town, you can have a tab at the grocery store, a tab at the feed co-op, a tab at the mechanic, at the hardware store, at the lumberyard (though not at the Dollar General). You walk into the lumberyard, tell them you're grabbing a two-by-four, and you walk back out. They put it on your tab. All of these relationships are what give rural communities their special character and worth. We know each other. We watch out for each other. We take care of each other. People are connected—for good or for ill—and those bonds of connectivity are often invisible to pastors or others coming in from the outside.

Cities have structure, too, circles of people with a shared history and identity. The difference is that in the city, the circles often intersect and overlap and no one circle can dominate the others. People move between the circles of structure, and new people are constantly arriving and destabilizing the historic hierarchies.

But in rural communities, the old structure is still present and visible. It's still load-bearing. And congregations embedded in and committed to it—congregations that previously derived strength from the old structure—in many cases now find themselves sagging under its weight. Churches are dying because of the old structure, pierced by its rusty edges as it collapses from out-migration due to economic opportunity and low birth rates.

Even as the old structure has grown dilapidated, new people have moved into rural communities, sometimes in waves as when powerful economic forces drive large population shifts, or sometimes individually as people seek what people always seek: safe neighborhoods, affordable housing, jobs, and good schools.

These structural shifts mean that for many rural communities, the demographic center of gravity has swung from the historic population to newcomers, and some old guard churches have experienced decline and gotten stuck. Enter the second way we make good on the bold hope of the resurrection in rural communities: church planting.

While organizations like the Rural Home Missionary Association have equipped rural church planters for years, and Village Missions has long sent pastors to serve remote congregations at risk of closing their doors because of finances or simply the challenge of finding a pastor, in the past decade, there's been a movement afoot to plant fresh expressions of church in rural communities. In 2018, the Acts 29 Network launched its Rural Collective. Despite its urban origin, the Gospel Coalition has drawn attention to rural church planting and sought to encourage up-and-coming leaders to consider rural. Regional outfits like Small Town Summits equip and encourage rural leaders across New England through workshops and networking. Some organizations focus on a particular province or state, like Vermont Church Planting.

At the same time, young, traditionally urban-centric networks like the Vineyard Movement have developed a strategy of planting congregations in the county seat of every rural county in the United States.[15] The much older Assemblies of God denomination has continuously established new congregations in deeply rural communities both by the organic spread of the Pentecostal movement and through a sustained vision for church planting.

Nearly all of the impassioned calls to rural church planting in the past few years have focused on demographic pragmatism. They go something like this: there are a lot of people living in rural communities in North America—more than in many countries—and they need Jesus too. Those arguments for going rural are true enough in their way, but they often neglect the multi-century witness of existing congregations. Rural North America is not an ecclesiological blank slate. It's difficult for leaders with a vision for rural church planting to avoid the same strategical calculations that dominate planting in urban and suburban environments. The question naturally turns to where a leader can make the most impact—an important consideration, but one that runs counter to the inherently nonstrategic location and nature of rural communities. There's always the risk that rural church planting becomes an exercise in overseeding, more about furthering our house brand than connecting with unreached peoples.

Nevertheless, there remain communities across North America still largely untouched by the gospel witness. Harrison Kwok and his wife founded The Northern Collective Church in the urban core of Whitehorse, Canada, a small city in the Yukon Territory. But their congregation's vision is to see thriving, gospel-centered churches in each of the nearly twenty communities of the Yukon. Many of them are First Nations communities and are relatively isolated. One community can only be reached by small plane. The challenges are complex, but the need is straightforward.[16]

Yet the greatest need—and perhaps the greatest challenge—for rural church planting comes from the kind of highly-structured rural communities I've been describing throughout this book. The old-name cemetery represents the deep roots of the community, and churches become a kind of Keeper of the Cemetery, literally and metaphorically. Those are our people, a century and a half of beloved ancestors, family names twining into the present. We pamper those ancient headstones. The grass is manicured. It's a labor of duty and love. A church I served paid my son to trim around the graves throughout the summer. Once, evening caught him finishing up his work after dark. I teased him when I swung by to pick him up. "Were you concerned to be in the cemetery at night?" I asked. "Nah," he said. "They're Mennonites." Our people.

That's the challenge, and why fresh expressions of church can make such a difference in rural communities. You see, within any rural community there are scads of folks who don't fit within the established structure, either because they've moved in from outside or because they've fallen afoul of the structure in some way. They're not "our people."

Charlie Cotherman, a church planter in small-town Oil City, Pennsylvania, speaks of the need for new churches that can "come alongside longstanding congregations for the common good."[17] In my opinion, the most powerful contribution to the common good that new churches can make is connecting with people who stand outside the existing structure of rural communities, people whose ancestors aren't buried in the church cemetery.

Pastors new to traditional rural congregations often grouse about how their efforts get stymied by complaints of *that's not the way we've always done it*. Alas, *not-the-way-we've-always-done-it-ism* will ring true for a lot of leaders. But a deeper dynamic than blind adherence to tradition is at work. To follow the old ways is to honor the structure of the community and congregation, and that is, perhaps, to honor those ancestors buried in the cemetery. They kept the faith. So do we.

The structure of rural communities makes these communities strong. It makes them resilient. Structure is about relationships. Structure gets things done. The realtor is the basketball coach is the scion of that big church family. Structure is about goodwill and influence. It's not easy to buck, because multiple parties have a vested interest in the ways things hold together. If you can learn to play ball within the lines of the community's structure, it can be powerful.

Or exclusive. The same structure that unites people across generations and neighborhoods, that bonds families and friends into the buried past, creates outsiders. The usual rifts are in play: skin color, marital status, economic standing, political affiliation. There's more than one way to otherize a cat. *You're not from around here, are you?* Sometimes, it's just that simple.

A pastor once told me about a visitor to his congregation. Shortly after arriving, the woman sized up the place and asked, "Can I be baptized here?" She was trying to envision it, make an imaginative leap. She knew the word—*baptize*—but what would it mean for her? What would it look like for her to be welcomed into the faith life of this particular community? Or something like that. She visited only a few times before disappearing. And she never did manage to get baptized there.

This is where the very structure of rural communities can lead to a Dead End. Outsiders cannot imagine themselves at the church. They know they won't fit. No one has to tell them. And so they don't stay long or don't show up at all.

In this way, new rural church plants can be an imaginative fresh start. They're a chance to renovate the imagination of the community, rejig the structure in a way that creates opportunities for new people to belong and have ownership. New rural church plants make it possible for someone to make the imaginative leap into a congregation.

Of course, rightly or wrongly, any disruption to the structure will be perceived as destructive by some within the community. There's the usual concern about "sheep stealing" among old guard congregations (not always entirely unjustified), but it runs deeper to a felt but often unnamed sense that the old, reliable ways of being together in the community are under threat—or at least being renegotiated in a discomfiting way.

Jim and Tina Von Wald planted New Life Church in Foley, Minnesota, in 2002. At that time, the community had a strong Lutheran and Catholic witness, but no evangelical or Pentecostal church. "What do we need another church for?" asked one community member as the Von Walds set to work. "We already have four." Another man, who would later connect to the church and become involved in leadership, confessed to the Von Walds how he and his friends sat at the bar and took bets on how long New Life would last.[18]

The congregation has not only lasted but thrived. In the years since its founding, New Life has grown to some 350 individuals gathering to worship on Sunday morning and a vibrant midweek kids program. The Von Walds intentionally worked not to target active churchgoers from the established congregations. Those folks included a large proportion of unchurched people, but also some cultural Lutherans and Catholics. They're people who may have been baptized as infants and hold vaguely Lutheran or Catholic imaginaries, but who largely never attended church. Pastors Jim and Tina describe Foley as a "closed community" at the time they arrived. They worked hard to contextualize their ministry and meet people where they were. For instance, in a nod to the predominant religious mores of Foley, the Von Walds developed first communion and confirmation services for children, though their Assemblies of God faith and practice do not traditionally call for either. Ministries like these geared toward children have been critical to the congregation's outreach. The family became deeply involved in the school by following their own kids, but also by volunteering and driving school buses. Jim coaches football and baseball in the high school. Tina said, "I would be a proponent in rural communities of planting a church because you determine how you're going to thrive, and if people don't like it, they don't come."

This may be the secret in a nutshell: a new church generates a new jag on the community's structure and gives people permission to locate themselves within it. It's not just that new church plants are doing something different that engages unchurched and dechurched people. Church plants rejigger the culture of a community in a way that allows more people to participate and thrive.

REVITALIZE

Is this sort of renewal only possible with a church plant? Could an old guard congregation pull off the same trick through savvy reinvention? I don't think old guard churches are off the hook. This is where the work of revitalization comes in. But it's hard to rebuild the boat while you're sailing it, which is why so few pastors manage to successfully lead their congregations in a revitalization process. The old structure of a church has to die for a fresh expression of church to rise. Understandably enough, most people find death too painful to face straight on and willingly.

Yet with steadfast leadership, some congregations do pull it off. Sometimes, the work of revitalization just means doing church well: repairing the building, equipping and encouraging the members, reaching out in the community. In this case, revitalization isn't a *thing*. It's just good leadership walking with an engaged congregation. The key skill is learning to see the church and community from God's perspective, with eyes for mission.

Tim Counts is a small-town Baptist pastor in Vermont.[19] When we spoke, Pastor Counts recalled how a number of years back he found himself led to pray "God, help me to see." He had moved across the country, from the Pacific Northwest to New England, landing in a congregation that had been prepped for growth by a capable and faithful former pastor who also happened to be Counts's mentor. But it was a new culture in a largely unreached state, and Counts struggled to know when his efforts were bearing fruit. He prayed that God would grant him to see angles for missions, to believe that God was working on people's hearts even when the numerical growth was not obvious. He needed God's help to see.

Under Counts's leadership, the congregation built a reputation for service. They didn't do anything heroic; they simply made some overdue changes to their grounds and went looking for ways to plug in to existing community events. The congregation put up a tent with a table for coffee, cookies, and gospel tracts at the community Easter egg hunt. They started a block party with carnival games and bouncy houses. Everybody left the party with a tract, a copy of the gospel of John, and an invitation to the church. They moved their vacation Bible school program from the church lawn to a nearby sports area in the park. That might seem like a counterintuitive move, but the congregation felt that they were reaching the heart of the community there. So many people participated in sports in the park, making it a welcoming and familiar place.

The church grew: spiritually, in its capacity for evangelism, in service and impact on the community. And over time: in numbers.

Sometimes, the necessary cultural change happens slowly. Glacially. The work of revitalization requires new ways of doing things among people who have shuffled in a long rut in the same direction for years. Not easily done. Without a bold hope for the resurrection, none of us would dare attempt any of it.

Our Easter faith shapes our lives around a hope that lies beyond us and touches the work that pastors and leaders dare undertake in the rural church. It's resurrection or bust. "It is critical," writes Eugene Peterson, "that we realize not just that the resurrection happened, but that it happens. Too often we make the resurrection only a matter of apologetics and melt the resurrection accounts down into an ingot of doctrine."[20] As James 2:19 states, "even the demons believe" that the resurrection happened. The resurrection was the pivotal moment in the history of their downfall and our salvation. But to believe that resurrection happens here in this place among these people—that's another matter entirely.

And yet that's our claim. We're people of resurrection hope standing always and impossibly at the stark naked stone of the tomb. He. Is. Not! Here. Christ works his resurrecting power in and through us. It happened. Resurrection happens.

8

Good News Everywhere

They went out and fled from the tomb, for terror and amazement had seized them. —Mark 16:8a

Rural is a place under the sky. There's sky everywhere, just so much of it. You don't even need to look up. Sun patches blue linen. Hawk perches on fence post, and the horizon stretches away foreverly.

At the end of the gospel of Mark, a horizon opens up. The women go to the tomb, and Jesus is not there because he has been raised and gone on ahead of them. As Mark 16:2 recounts, it is "very early on the first day of the week." The stone is rolled back, the tomb opens to the sky, and the message of the angel is "go" (v. 7). The first women flee from that vastness, heading toward a horizon they do not know, "for terror and amazement had seized them." They are silent in the face of a mystery they cannot comprehend (v. 8).

I keep finding myself in this place in the rural church, this big sky expanse where I am seized by terror and amazement, brought to wordlessness. Where am I? What am I doing here? But in my best moments, rural's big sky tugs on something behind my belly button, and I feel *it*: that-hello-where-have-you-been-always-right-here-above-and-below-you terror and

amazement (literally in the Greek: "trembling and ecstasy").
And that's what I think we have to operate from and get back
to when we lose our way. Jesus goes ahead of us and ministers
through us in rural places, and our truest response is trembling
reverence before the work and *ekstasis*—amazement—that we
get to be a part of it.

TREMBLING

The women are afraid, and it brings them to silence, which
is the only proper response to finding that the bars of death
have been broken clean through. "Be still, and know that I am
God," says Psalm 46:10. The fear of the Lord is the beginning
of wisdom for them.

But before Mark writes of fear, he writes that "terror and
amazement had seized them" (Mark 16:8). In the Greek, the
first word is actually "trembling." It rides shotgun with "fear"
many times in the Scriptures, but not the cowardly type of fear.
Trembling has notes of reverence. "Work out your salvation
with fear and trembling" says Paul (Philippians 2:12 NIV).
When God saved his people out of Egypt, the nations froze
in "fear and trembling" (Exodus 15:16 in the Greek version
of the OT). "Fear and trembling come upon me, and horror
overwhelms me," reads Psalm 55:5.

There at dawning of Jesus' revolution, the women trembled. They were awed to silence. Everything else begins with
that, right there. They trembled before the empty tomb.

Christ infuses ministry with a sacredness that calls for
silence, calls for fear of the Lord, calls for trembling. It's all too
easy to lose sight of that truth in rural ministry. I've seen it. I've
felt it. We come to the work with a sense of (what exactly?)—
some therapeutic modality, some interventionism, maybe even

a little despair, because the church and community are so small out there under that wide, wide sky. And who are we?

But this is Christ's ministry, and on this new day under this wide sky, Jesus didn't wait at the tomb. He went ahead to Galilee, and we are left to catch up yet again. Because Jesus is doing it through us, this ministry we're given is a real thing. Rural and small-town congregations aren't miniature suburban churches or failed megachurches, they're their own animal, and it's a wild kind of mastodon thing that's not terrified to lift up its head under that big sky. You have to respect rural ministry just for the audacity it takes to go there and do it.

But more importantly, we have to take to heart that it's Jesus' ministry we're engaged in. "Carry out your ministry fully," writes Paul in 2 Timothy 4:5. So let's. Come with a sacred, trembling awe to the fact of the rural church. Jesus' ministry in rural places, society's far ends of the earth, is good news everywhere because it means that God really does love the whole world. If those little steepled specks on the horizon matter, then everywhere does. Cities are just bigger specks in the cosmic sweep, just more aggregate dust. And God really does love it all.

And so as pastors and leaders, we accompany rural congregations and communities with reverent trembling. We come to them as they are: isolated, sparse, distant—recalcitrantly rural. The people don't need to be fixed by moving them to a bigger place with more economic opportunities or something. In fact, if rural places didn't exist, we would re-create them. The human heart is always yearning for the farther horizon. If it weren't rural Kansas or rural Texas or rural Saskatchewan, it would be rural Olympus Mons or something. Humanity will always have a rural edge.

At the farther horizon, that rural and small-town place, believe you can do much. Love on the school, start the youth program, run for mayor. I've met—and I admire—pastors and leaders who have found ways to get outside and do these things. My sin is always an uninspired variation on the same theme: getting stuck inside a little shelter built of to-do lists.

Even then, faithful witness is more than community involvement. There are currents at work that want to minimize rural communities and small towns, and we can unwittingly play along. Sometimes the most faithful thing we can do is lead from reverence. Reverent leadership honors the integrity of rural people and places and keeps us grounded as leaders. Reverence is our sign of contradiction (cf. Luke 2:34). Reverence reminds us that the work is the Lord's.[1]

The risk of foregrounding community involvement is that we can fall into the temptation to make something happen. In my earliest days as a minister, the parsonage and church stood at the bottom of a residential hill in our little town. On Sunday afternoons, after preaching to the usual sparse crowd for morning worship, you could find me staring longingly up the hill at all those houses with all those people who, whatever little else I may have known about them, did not attend my church—maybe any church. I knocked on a few of their doors over the years, and some of them responded positively and invited me in and even showed up in church. But I wonder whether on those Sunday afternoons, I ought to have listened to G. K. Chesterton and given "room for good things to run wild."[2] I ought to have watched my son pedal circles on his bike. Or taken a nap. In short, just received the gift of myself in that place. (You'll get this, or you won't). A certain trembling comes when we're present to the fullness of something. It may be that the most important thing we do is show up and follow Jesus' lead. It's flat advice to say, "Just love the people." I won't tell you that. But somehow you have to learn to be where you are for real. Jesus has gone ahead of us to Galilee. He's doing what he wants to do. Let's take that to heart in the rural church.

AMAZEMENT

Jesus departed the tomb, and the women froze in "amazement" (Mark 16:8). The word in Greek is *ekstasis*, which implies being levered out of one's usual frame of mind. Get out of your head. When Jesus unexpectedly both forgave sins and healed the body of the paralytic who came through the roof, an "*ekstasis* seized all of them" (Luke 5:26). In Abram's vision quest, an "*ekstasis* fell upon Abram, and a deep and terrifying darkness descended upon him" (Genesis 15:12). The apostle Peter was praying on the rooftop when he fell into an *ekstasis* and saw the great smorgasbordian sheet of the new regime unfurling before him (Acts 10:10–15). *Ekstasis* is wow! (with the exclamation mark). It's a gasp of delight. I didn't know life could do that.

The new horizon of the empty tomb opens up under *ekstasis*. This is true of all of Christian life, the surprise of the resurrection here and here and right over there. The Living One shows up. Do you see his wounds? Wow! But *ekstasis* amazement especially marks the gift and calling of ministry, nowhere more so than in the rural and small-town church. Rural ministry is ecstatic.

Hear me out. So often, rural ministry is framed by need: God or the people or the church need you, and you should go, and you should do it, and you should learn to like it. There are *should*s everywhere. Rural ministry becomes a response to all that shouldful need.

Which appeals to something within a lot of us: the almost military longing to go to hard places and do hard things and bleed a little. During an interview to be pastor of a church, I once told the church, in complete earnestness, that my wife and I strive to live simply and with less, that we were actually trying to go down the financial ladder. They offered to help. But I probably would have impressed Freud more than Chrysostom.

My own Anabaptist/Mennonite tradition contains an undercurrent of redemptive suffering, a martyr complex even, that traces back to the beginnings. Early leaders spoke of the need to follow the "Bitter Christ" rather than some peoples' easy faith-alone and let's have a drink "Sweet Christ."[3] It takes no leap of the imagination to intuit what follows: a bitter Christ calls forth a bitter ministry. After all, Jesus commissioned his greatest apostle ever with the words "I myself will show him how much he must suffer for the sake of my name" (Acts 9:16). We're the lamb in the thicket, the church that suffers, still "completing what is lacking in Christ's afflictions for the sake of his body" (Colossians 1:24). It's the cross all the way down.

Even so, Christ has more for us. I once was driving with a seasoned pastor, now gone on to glory, who told me his ministry story. He had been called to a big historical church out in the middle of the wheatfields just as some generational fault lines began to rumble. He employed all his best giftings and empathy and struggling prayers, but the church fissured, and he ended up in therapy. At some point, his therapist told him, "You need a ministry you can enjoy."

I sat up when he told me this. A ministry he could enjoy? I didn't know you could ask for that.

So I'm learning to receive the good gifts of ministry. I'm not an easy one to give gifts to. I doubt the gifts and question whether I deserve them. But I've been having these little *ekstasis* jabs of amazement at the goodness of ministry in these rural and small-town places, and I think that's part of what we have to learn to receive. There's a joy here. Rural ministry can do that.

It sometimes takes folks from outside to help us see the goodness. A beaten-down pastor from another tradition took refuge for a while in a church I was serving. The fact of his coming back, Sunday after Sunday, and finding nourishment and faith, let me recognize the gifts I was living daily. Some visitors from New York City came to town and took pictures of our farmer's market. Are you seeing this? I was just there to pick up a couple of shiny zucchinis.

In Mark 16:8, when trembling and *ekstasis* seize the women, they don't do anything. They don't say anything. They're just there. It's not even clear they've understood what is happening. There's no self-improvement or self-help, no strategy. Jesus is already out and away doing his thing. The resurrection will not be instrumentalized. The story does not resolve in verse 8, it opens up. Take it or leave it. That's the first way the gospel ends.

Of course, our version of the gospel has more: "shorter" (v. 8b) and "longer" (vv. 9–20) endings. A standard explanation of these additions is that the church was dissatisfied with Mark's first, abrupt ending, or maybe even the actual ending was lost in the church's scrappy early years. And so someone— or various someones—cribbed Matthew and Luke (who had earlier cribbed Mark) and stapled a few further paragraphs to Mark's dangling gospel.

I'm struck that there might be another way to interpret the presence of the additional endings. Perhaps they were indeed added. But they were added to prove and document what

Mark was trying to tell us all along: Jesus just keeps right on making up his ministry in and through his church. Because Jesus is with them, "signs will accompany" his people. They'll "speak in new tongues." They'll pick up snakes. They'll drink down death—and yet live. They'll pray for the sick, and the sick will be healed (vv. 17–18). "The Lord worked with them and confirmed the message by the signs that accompanied it" (v. 20).

That's the ecstatic surprise and promise of rural ministry. Jesus is still creating something new and good. Christ walks with us "into the country" (v. 12). He keeps insisting on sending us out onto the highways and podunk byways, a people bearing his name in every flyover Galilee. "They went out and proclaimed the good news everywhere," ends verse 20. They walked out under that new sky, seized by Jesus' nail-bright love.

Acknowledgments

To my wife and sons for giving me the space and grace to write.

To the congregations I have served, for your faithfulness as we have walked over hills and through valleys during these years. Together, we have cultivated test plots that have shaped my thinking and growth in what it means to be a rural pastor.

To pastors and leaders across the continent who graciously took time to share your wisdom.

Soli Deo gloria!

Notes

CHAPTER 1

1. See "How Does the US Census Bureau Define Rural?," accessed March 31, 2024, https://mtgis-portal.geo.census.gov/arcgis/apps/storymaps/collections/189aa1dbd64c4c81b3b4a2b71124f6c6?item=1.

2. "Canada Goes Urban," Statistics Canada, last modified May 17, 2018, https://www150.statcan.gc.ca/n1/pub/11-630-x/11-630-x2015004-eng.htm.

3. Bakhtiar Moazzami, "Fewer and Older: Population and Demographic Challenges across Rural Canada, 2015," Strengthening Rural Canada, last modified April 24, 2021, http://www.decoda.ca/wp-content/uploads/Fewer-Older-Population-and-Demographic-Challenges-Across-Rural-Canada.pdf.

4. Robert Wuthnow, *Left Behind: Decline and Rage in Small-Town America* (Princeton: Princeton University Press, 2018), 11.

5. See Aaron Earls, "The Church Growth Gap: The Big Get Bigger while the Small Get Smaller," *Christianity Today*, March 6, 2019, https://www.christianitytoday.com/news/2019/march/lifeway-research-church-growth-attendance-size.html.

6. "Who Is a Democrat: Democratic Voters Are Less Liberal than Party Activists Think They Are," *The Economist*, July 12, 2018, https://www.economist.com/special-report/2018/07/12/who-is-a-democrat.

7. Ed Pilkington, "Obama Angers Midwest Votes with Guns and Religion Remark," *The Guardian*, April 14, 2008.

8. See Brad Roth, *God's Country: Faith, Hope, and the Future of the Rural Church* (Harrisonburg, VA: Herald Press, 2017), 25–26. In 2020, the US Census upped its rural threshold to five thousand.

9. "New Census Data Show Differences between Urban and Rural Populations," United States Census Bureau, December 8, 2016, https://www.census.gov/newsroom/press-releases/2016/cb16-210.html.

10. "Our Community," Garden City, accessed March 5, 2024, https://www.garden-city.org/our-community.

11. Wuthnow, *Left Behind*. Wuthnow uses the language of revered father of sociology Émile Durkheim.

12. "History: Urban and Rural," United States Census Bureau, accessed January 14, 2024, https://www.census.gov/history/www/programs/geography/urban_and_rural_areas.html.

13. Nicholas F. Jacobs and Daniel M. Shea, *The Rural Voter: The Politics of Place and the Disuniting of America* (New York: Columbia University Press, 2024), 13. See especially chapter 2.

14. See Matthew 13:52.

15. Harold Senkbeil, *The Care of Souls: Cultivating a Pastor's Heart* (Bellingham, WA: Lexham Press), xx.

16. Eugene Peterson, *Christ Plays in Ten Thousand Places: A Conversation in Spiritual Theology* (Grand Rapids, MI: Eerdmans, 2005), 273, 231.

17. Kate Shellnutt, "Small Town Pastors See More Than Small Wonders," *Christianity Today* 63, no. 2 (2019), 16.

CHAPTER 2

1. Ernest Heminway, "A Clean, Well-Lighted Place," in *The Short Stories: The First Forty-Nine Stories with a Brief Preface by the Author* (New York: Scribner, 1995), 379–83.

2. Thomas H. Johnson, ed., *The Complete Poems of Emily Dickinson* (New York: Little, Brown, and Company, 1960), 294.

3. Anthony Lane, "The Disappearing Poet: Whatever Happened to Weldon Kees?," *New Yorker*, July 4, 2005, https://www.newyorker.com/magazine/2005/07/04/the-disappearing-poet.

4. Carl Sandburg, "Chicago," in *Chicago Poems: Unabridged* (Mineola, NY: Dover, 1994), 1.

5. This and following paragraph reprinted from Brad Roth, "Rural American Faces the Abyss," *Harvard Divinity Bulletin* 48, no. 1–2 (Spring/Summer 2020): 17. Used with permission.

6. See US Census statistics compiled at "Jewell County, Kansas Population," World Population Review, accessed January 31, 2024, https://worldpopulationreview.com/us-counties/ks/jewell-county-population.

7. Donnie Griggs, *Small Town Jesus: Taking the Gospel Mission Seriously in Seemingly Unimportant Places* (Damascus, MD: EverTruth, 2016), 131.

8. Timothy Fry and Timothy Horner, trans., *The Rule of St. Benedict in English* (Collegeville, MN: Liturgical Press, 1981), 64:16–18.

9. Eugene Peterson, *Under the Unpredictable Plant: An Exploration in Vocational Holiness* (Grand Rapids: Eerdmans, 1992), 160–61.

10. On highways to Zion, see Psalm 84:5.

11. Pete Grieg, *How to Pray: A Simple Guide for Normal People* (Colorado Springs, CO: NavPress, 2019), 162.

12. Stephen Witmer, *A Big Gospel in Small Places: Why Ministry in Forgotten Communities Matters* (Downers Grove, IL: InterVarsity Press, 2019), 10.

13. Kevin O'Brien, *The Ignatian Adventure: Experiencing the Spiritual Exercises of Saint Ignatius in Daily Life* (Chicago: Loyola Press, 2011), 176.

14. See John 21:11.

15. See Mark 1:11–13 and 2 Corinthians 4:7.

16. James Martin, "Magis," Ignatian Spirituality, July 13, 2018, https://www.ignatianspirituality.com/magis/.

17. This and following paragraph reprinted from Brad Roth, "*Magis* with Less," *Leader*, Fall 2019, © 2019 MennoMedia. Used with permission.

18. Conversation with author, September 21, 2017.
19. See Brad Roth, "Just Don't Call It 'Social Justice': In Rural Communities, Churches Engage in Practical and Compassionate Ministries to Empower Others for the Common Good," *Sojourners*, December 2018, https://sojo.net/magazine/december-2018/just-dont-call-it-social-justice-rural-ministry.
20. Karl Vaters, *Small Church Essentials: Field-Tested Principles for Leading a Healthy Congregation of Under 250* (Chicago: Moody Publishers, 2018), 19.

CHAPTER 3

1. David Platt, *Follow Me: A Call to Die, A Call to Life* (Carol Stream, IL: Tyndale House, 2013), 208.
2. *Encyclopedia Britannica Online*, s.v. "Second Great Awakening," accessed February 25, 2024, https://www.britannica.com/topic/Second-Great-Awakening.
3. See J. Todd Billings, *Remembrance, Communion, and Hope: Rediscovering the Gospel at the Lord's Table* (Grand Rapids, MI: Eerdmans, 2018), loc. 1193 of 5133, Kindle.
4. Benson Y. Landis, *Rural Church Life in the Middle West* (New York: George H. Doran Company, 1922), 55.
5. James K. A. Smith, *Imagining the Kingdom: How Worship Works* (Grand Rapids, MI: Baker Academic, 2013), 81.
6. Alan Kreider, *The Patient Ferment of the Early Church: The Improbable Rise of Christianity in the Roman Empire* (Grand Rapids, MI: Baker Academic, 2016), 74.
7. Ed Cyzewski, *Flee, Be Silent, Pray: Ancient Prayers for Anxious Christians* (Harrisonburg, VA: Herald Press, 2019), 59.
8. Author interview, December 1, 2020.
9. Sarah Melotte, "Rural People Don't Practice Religion More Than Their Urban Counterparts, Survey Shows," *Daily Yonder*, October 23, 2023, https://dailyyonder.com/rural-people-dont-practice-religion-more-than-their-urban-counterparts-survey-shows/2023/10/23/.
10. Conversation with author, June 8, 2018.

CHAPTER 4

1. Chimamanda Ngozi Adichie, "The Danger of a Single Story," TED talk, July 2009, https://www.ted.com/talks/chimamanda_ngozi_adichie_the_danger_of_a_single_story.
2. Max De Pree, quoted in Karl Vaters, *Small Church Essentials: Field-Tested Principles for Leading a Healthy Congregation of Under 250* (Chicago: Moody Publishers, 2018), 72.
3. Quoted in "Wine and Bottles: The Fruity Lexicon of Wine Suggests the Links Between Language and Understanding," *The Economist* 437, no. 9216 (2020): 73.
4. Stephen Witmer, *A Big Gospel in Small Places: Why Ministry in Forgotten Places Matters* (Downers Grove, IL: InterVarsity Press, 2019), 77. Emphasis original.
5. Philip Thibodeau, *Playing the Farmer: Representations of Rural Life in Vergil's Georgics* (Berkeley and Los Angeles: University of California Press, 2011), 76.
6. Frederick Buechner, *The Remarkable Ordinary: How to Stop, Look, and Listen to Life* (Grand Rapids, MI: Zondervan, 2017), 18, 22. Italics original.
7. C. S. Lewis, *The Horse and His Boy* (New York: HarperCollins, 2000), 165.
8. Benjamin Winchester, "A Rural Brain Gain Migration," University of Minnesota Extension, https://extension.umn.edu/economic-development/

rural-brain-gain-migration. What's more, because of their very growth, some communities have classed out of rural and been redesignated. See Jan Pytalski, "Report: Rural Counties' Being Reclassified as Urban Can Mask Their Successes," *Daily Yonder*, December 11, 2020, https://dailyyonder.com/report-rural-counties-being-reclassified-as-urban-can-mask-their-successes/2020/12/11/.

9. Kristin Tate, "Americans Leave Large Cities for Suburban Areas and Rural Towns," *The Hill*, July 5, 2020, https://thehill.com/opinion/finance/505944-americans-leave-large-cities-for-suburban-areas-and-rural-towns.

10. See Ellen Barry, "The Virus Sent Droves to a Small Town, Suddenly It's Not So Small," *New York Times*, September 26, 2020, https://www.nytimes.com/2020/09/26/us/coronavirus-vermont-transplants.html.

11. Patricia Middleton, "Growing Population in Some Small Towns," *McPherson Sentinel*, January 12, 2018, http://www.mcphersonsentinel.com/news/20180112/growing-population-in-some-small-towns.

12. Nicholas F. Jacobs and Daniel M. Shea, *The Rural Voter: The Politics of Place and the Disuniting of America* (New York: Columbia University Press, 2024), 13.

13. Annie Dillard, "Pilgrim at Tinker Creek," in *The Annie Dillard Reader* (New York: HarperCollins, 1994), 287.

CHAPTER 5

1. "Fail Often, Fail Well: Companies Have a Great Deal to Learn from Failure—Provided They Manage It Successfully," *The Economist*, April 14, 2011, https://www.economist.com/business/2011/04/14/fail-often-fail-well.

2. Astro Teller, "The Unexpected Benefit of Celebrating Failure," TED talk, February 2016, accessed November 27, 2020, https://www.ted.com/talks/astro_teller_the_unexpected_benefit_of_celebrating_failure.

3. Joel Marcus, *Mark 1–8: A New Translation with Introduction and Commentary (The Anchor Bible)* (New York: Doubleday, 2000), 426.

4. Deborah E. Gorton, *Embracing Uncomfortable: Facing Our Fears While Pursuing Our Purpose* (Chicago: Northfield Publishing, 2020), 151.

5. Author interview, November 17, 2020.

6. Teller, "Unexpected Benefits of Celebrating Failure."

7. J. R. Briggs, *Fail: Finding Hope and Grace in the Midst of Ministry Failure* (Downers Grove, IL: InterVarsity Press, 2014), 44.

8. Author interview, November 24, 2020.

9. Briggs, *Fail*, 22.

10. Author interview, June 3, 2018.

11. See Kennedy Smith, "How Do You Buy Groceries When There's No Grocery Store? These Communities Figured It Out," *Daily Yonder*, November 13, 2023, https://dailyyonder.com/how-do-you-buy-groceries-when-theres-no-grocery-store-these-communities-figured-it-out/2023/11/13/.

12. See John Piper, *Adoniram Judson: How Few There Are Who Die So Hard!* (Minneapolis: Desiring God Foundation, 2012).

13. Greg Fromhoz, director, *Peterson: In Between the Man and the Message* (Carol Stream, IL: NavPress, August 30, 2016), accessed December 1, 2020: https://www.youtube.com/watch?v=LaMgIvbXqSk.

14. George Lucas, *Return of the Jedi* (Hollywood, CA: Lucasfilm Ltd., 1983).

15. Author interview, November 18, 2020..

CHAPTER 6

1. Eugene H. Peterson, *Working the Angles: The Shape of Pastoral Integrity* (Grand Rapids, MI: Eerdmans, 1987, reprinted 2000), 2.
2. John Calvin, *Institutes of Christian Religion*, John T. McNeill, ed., Ford Lewis Battles, trans. (Philadelphia: Westminster Press, 1960) 4.1.9., 1023.
3. Burying the dead features as a work of mercy in the book of Tobit in the Apocrypha. See Pontifical Council for the Promotion of the New Evangelization, *The Corporal and Spiritual Works of Mercy* (Huntington, IN: Our Sunday Visitor Publishing Division, 2015), 46.
4. Pontifical Council, 49–50.
5. Ed Stetzer and Thom Rainer, *Transformational Church: Creating a Scorecard for Congregations* (Nashville: B&H Publishing Group, 2010), 26.
6. Gil Rendle, *Doing the Math of Mission: Fruits, Faithfulness, and Metrics* (Lanham, MD: Rowman and Littlefield, 2014), 2.
7. Stetzer and Rainer, *Transformational Church*, 29.
8. This paragraph is adapted from Brad Roth, "Seeing through to a Cruciform Incarnationality," in *Sapientia*, December 7, 2020, https://henrycenter.tiu.edu/2020/12/seeing-through-to-a-cruciform-incarnationality/. Used by permission.
9. See Jerry Z. Muller, *The Tyranny of Metrics* (Princeton, NJ: Princeton University Press, 2018), 24.
10. Muller, 32.
11. Author interview, November 17, 2020.
12. Timothy Fry and Timothy Horner, trans., *The Rule of St. Benedict in English* (Collegeville, MN: Liturgical Press, 1981), 26–29.
13. Fry and Horner, 95–96.
14. Andy Crouch, "A Rule of Life for Redemptive Entrepreneurs," *Faith Driven Entrepreneur*, audio podcast, March 6, 2019, https://www.faithdrivenentrepreneur.org/blog/2019/3/27/a-rule-of-life-for-redemptive-entrepreneurs.
15. Stephen A. Macchia, *Crafting a Rule of Life: An Invitation to the Well-Ordered Way* (Downers Grove, IL: InterVarsity Press, 2012), 14.
16. See I. Howard Marshall, *The Gospel of Luke: A Commentary on the Greek Text*, New International Greek Testament Commentary (Grand Rapids, MI: Eerdmans, 1978), 644.
17. Rendle, *Doing the Math of Mission*, 66.
18. Quoted in Bonnie Thurston, *Hidden in God: Discovering the Desert Vision of Charles de Foucauld* (Notre Dame, IN: Ave Maria Press, 2016), 103.
19. For this section I rely on Thurston, *Hidden in God*.
20. Thurston, 93.
21. Thurston, 24.
22. Thurston, preface.

CHAPTER 7

1. "Fragments from a Forgotten Valley: Three Months in the Life of a French Village Reveals that Isolation Can Mean Solace as Well as Hardship," *The Economist* 437, no. 9225 (December 19, 2020): 31.

2. See 1 Kings 17:17–24; 2 Kings 4:17–37; Luke 7:11–17; John 11:38–44.

3. See Luke 4:23.

4. See John 20:7.

5. See 2 Kings 6:5–7; Joshua 10:13; Numbers 22:28.

6. Rowan Williams, *The Way of St Benedict* (London: Bloomsbury Continuum, 2020), 27.

7. See Mark 1:14, 16, 39.

8. See John 2:1–11; Mark 2:1–12.

9. Mark 14:28; 16:7.

10. See Romans 15:28.

11. Author interview, December 8, 2020.

12. Timothy Fry and Timothy Horner, trans., *The Rule of St. Benedict in English* (Collegeville, MN: Liturgical Press, 1981), 29.

13. Nate Klug, *Anyone* (Chicago: University of Chicago Press, 2015), 50.

14. Charles Wesley, "Oh for a Thousand Tongues to Sing," in Rebecca Slough, ed., *Hymnal: A Worship Book* (Scottdale, PA: Mennonite Publishing House, 1992), 110.

15. Author interview with Michael Houle of Small Town USA / Multiply Vineyard, January 28, 2021.

16. Conversation with author, January 11, 2021. Pastor Harrison is also profiled at "Rural Profile: Meet Harrison and Kaitlyn Kwok," *Acts 29*, August 6, 2020, https://www.acts29.com/rural-profile-meet-harrison-and-kaitlyn-kwok/.

17. Charlie Cotherman, "A Love Song for the Rural Church," *Sapientia*, December 2, 2020, https://henrycenter.tiu.edu/2020/12/a-love-song-for-the-rural-church/.

18. Author interview, December 31, 2020.

19. Author interview, November 19, 2020.

20. Eugene Peterson, *Christ Plays in Ten Thousand Places: A Conversation in Spiritual Theology* (Grand Rapids, MI: Eerdmans, 2005), 231.

CHAPTER 8

1. See Psalm 127; 1 Corinthians 15:58.

2. G. K. Chesterton, *Orthodoxy*, Christian Heritage Series (Moscow, ID: Canon Press, 2020), 101. First published 1908.

3. Robert Friedmann, "Sweet or Bitter Christ," *Global Anabaptist Mennonite Encyclopedia Online*, 1959, accessed January 4, 2024, https://gameo.org/index.php?title=Sweet_or_Bitter_Christ&oldid=162915.

The Author

Brad Roth is a pastor in rural central Kansas. He grew up baling hay, tending sheep, and shearing Christmas trees on a farm in Illinois. He is a graduate of Augustana College, Harvard Divinity School, and Anabaptist Mennonite Biblical Seminary. Brad has a heart for serving God and God's people in rural communities. He is passionate about sharing faith in word and deed and living out God's love in the community. He and his wife enjoy getting outside, tending a garden, and hanging out with their three sons.

www.ingramcontent.com/pod-product-compliance
Lightning Source LLC
Chambersburg PA
CBHW021149160426
42812CB00078B/275